Life After College

WORK AND THE ART OF LIVING

Stephen B. Sloane

ISBN: 1532743289

ISBN 13: 9781532743283

Library of Congress Control Number: 2016908804

CreateSpace Independent Publishing Platform

North Charleston, South Carolina

For Nicholas

Remember, the point of life is to be happy. All other goals (money, fame, status, responsibility, achievement) are merely ways of making you happy. They are worthless in themselves.

David H. Maister True Professionalism

There are two types of education. One should teach us how to make a living and the other how to live.

John Adams

But we must not forget that only a very few people are artists in life; that the art of life is the most distinguished and rarest of all the arts.

Carl Jung

Contents

Chapter One

Introduction

Social life involves being sorted by a few others who have, by the rest of us been given the power to sort. Our illusion is that it ends on graduation, from one school to another, when one teacher passes us, and then passes us on.But it never really does. We go on being driven and sorted until at last we're sorted out.......

Adam Gopnik, New Yorker Magazine Feb 2, 2015)

For it is for the sake of the end that all else is done.

Aristotle, Nicomachean Ethics

Every spring around 2 million people graduate from college. At thousands of graduation ceremonies *Very Important Personages* address the graduates with words of congratulations and advice. Champaign corks pop. Thumbs dance across smart phones in a ballet of texting excitement. Arms stretch from inside academic gowns to record *selfies*. Yawns appear on the faces of faculty who are thinking about a summer free of classroom duties. Nobody is paying attention.

Hovering above the spring sunshine of commencement day is the dark cloud of the next day, the first day of life after college. If this cloud could sing it would echo the voices of the 1950's rock and roll group *The Silhouettes* singing the doo-wop hit song *Get a Job.*

> Get a job Sha na na na, sha na na na na
> Every morning about this time
> She gets me out of my bed
> A-crying get a job.
> After breakfast, everyday,
> She throws the want ads right my way
> And never fails to say,
> Get a job Sha na na na, sha na na na na

Instead of thinking about the boring words of the VIP's speech or the picture of the dark cloud painted by the *sha na na* singers, imagine Shakespeare's voice in his play *Hamlet* uttering from the lips of Polonius his advice to his son Laertes, " This above all: To thine own self be true. And it must follow, as the night the day, thou canst not then be false to any man."

Imagine Aristotle's voice coming from ancient Greece telling graduates that "For it is for the sake of the end that all else is done"[1] thereby informing the graduates that happiness results from activity pursued as an end in and of itself rather than a means to an end. Then fast forward to Herman Wouk's novel *The Caine Mutiny*[2] and listen to the words of the dying father of Willie Keith, himself a recent graduate, advising Willie to find his "natural work," work that is satisfying in and of itself. Next, think about Ivan Ilych, as described by the voice of Leo Tolstoy in his novel *The Death of Ivan Ilych.*[3] Just as Willie Keith's father does, as he faces death, Ivan become conscious of the fact that he has lived a life not worth living.This understanding comes when it is too late to change sad reality. The twentieth century physician (Keith) and the nineteenth century lawyer (Ilych) have failed to understand Socrates' admonition that the examined life is the only life worth living.

Now shift gears and pay attention to the contradictory ideas proposed by those who have studied the process of work itself, ideas that are still accepted, in one form or another, by those who will control the working lives of graduates. Listen to Frederick Taylor[4], the very first management consultant, who proposed that the job of the manager was to find the one best way to accomplish a task and then make sure employees act in that way. Don't ignore the genius of Charlie Chaplain whose film *Modern Times*[5] depicts a manager who bought off on Taylor's idea of *scientific management* and attempts to feed his employees rapidly with a choking feeding machine to shorten time off for lunch and thereby increase efficiency. Listen to the voices of Elton Mayo[6] and his fellow Harvard based researchers who contradicted Taylor by finding that employee productivity was not the result of following the one best way mandated by managers. These fellows tell us that productivity is the result of the perception that the workplace is a social system where managers should understand that the satisfaction of human needs results in efficient production and that working groups conform to the informal rules established by the group rather than the formal rules specified by mangers. Then pay attention to William Whyte who warns us in his book *The Organization Man*[7] that when we think of our role as employees as parts of a social system, when we conform unquestioningly to the codes of behavior of the organization as a group, we risk the destruction of our individuality.

As you read the following chapters imagine the ignored words uttered from graduation day platforms and the foreboding demands of the *sha na na* rock and rollers being replaced by voices that leap from the pages of this book, voices that speak of philosophy, literature, history, drama, and science, voices which transcend the hollow words of *Very Important Personages* and the fearful admonition of the *doo-wop* singers, voices that stimulate, inform, and encourage graduates to live a life after college dominated by the purpose of pursuing the elusive goal of happiness where success depends not so much on finding a job as discovering one's own authentic self, of getting in touch with one's own soul.

Recently I taught a class titled *Life After Graduation* to seniors and juniors at the college where I have served as a member of the faculty for nearly thirty years since retiring from my career as a naval officer. I disguised the course with what I conceived to be a seductive name because in past years the abstract and theoretical nature of the material I planned to present discouraged students from enrolling and low enrollment meant that this year the course might be cancelled.

My field of academic expertise deals with social science and psychological concepts and theories which focus on explaining the activity of modern organizations and the behavior of the people who participate in organizational activity. I have been particularly interested in the study of organizations from a critical perspective that examines the power motivation of managers as it comes into conflict with the human needs of workers to control their own lives, a point of view that recognizes that the purposes of organizations do not always coincide with the human purposes of employees, an approach that explores the way that people are thought of and treated as human resources rather than human beings.

Students are justifiably fearful as they anticipate staying afloat in the not always genial currents and cross currents of organizational life once they leave the nurturing environment of *Alma Mater*. The real and not necessarily pleasant complications of the working world, particularly those which involve problems considered by a professor interested in a critical perspective, are matters students understandably prefer avoid as long as possible. The critical and less than encouraging ideas which explain the real and at times dark side of the working world would not serve to assuage students' fear of an uncertain and potentially stormy future. A course titled *A Critical Exploration of Complex Organizations* would not be high on the list of student course selection preference. This is particularly true today when many graduates are burdened with a heavy debt incurred as a result of expensive tuition and living costs, when immediate employment of prestigious well paying jobs is rare, when an undergraduate degree is as much of a ticket to economic benefit as a high school diploma used to be, and where the demanding words of the rock and roll singers noted above echo loud and clear.

On the other hand, a course title something like *Life After College* would create the impression, albeit a distorted one, that the planned course would provide simple easy to use practical *how to* tools and tactics that students might one day use to navigate the narrow channels of organizational reality and confidently sail into a safe harbor of economic security and happiness.

The ethics of the academic legerdemain, i.e. inventing a course title for the purpose of seducing students to enroll, did not bother me at all. I believed that I had something to say that would be useful to students and that I was seducing them into something that was worth the astronomical cost of tuition.

My *Machiavellian* strategy worked. With a Registrar imposed limit of twenty two students (my college prides itself on small classes) the enrollment filled up quickly and an impressive waiting list guaranteed full enrollment even if some would opt for an early dropping of the course. The Registrar was even persuaded by some clever student to increase the enrollment to a hefty twenty three.

I designed the course to include a number of case studies in the form of films, novels, my own research, and my own working experience. These narratives would form the grist for the mill of student analysis as well as my own use of theory and concepts that would explain the action and outcomes of the cases.

Once we got started, something *remarkable* happened. As we considered and analyzed the course cases and as I taught each session based on where we had gone the day before rather than on a predetermined course syllabus and daily lesson plan, the course took on a life of its own. This centered around themes and messages that had neither been anticipated by the students nor planned by myself. The course was no longer the originally planned purely academic exploration of a critical theoretical take on organizational life. The course did not evolve into a detailed prescribed easy to read road map to a smooth transition into the world of work that the students craved. The *teaching-learning* point of the course morphed as it came to focus on the notion that a life well lived is one experienced as a journey of discovery, the discovery of one's authentic self, and that happiness depends on the capacity to choose a path which is determined by the essence of that self.

Students and teacher examined and discussed course material which included descriptions of real and artfully described working lives of real and artfully imagined people as well as academic concepts that might help to understand the meaning of these lives. It became evident that a journey of self discovery does not result in a desired final destination. At best, the journey of self discovery takes twists and turns. At best, a person who takes Socrates advice to live an examined life[8] moves *toward* the knowledge of self. At best, the process of navigating the narrow channel that defines the twists and turns of a working life empowers a person to become increasingly able to pursue goals that are ends in and of themselves, to evade the *get a job* black cloud, to pursue the *blue bird of happiness.*

As the course progressed, we learned that a journey of self discovery should depend on a continuous process of understanding what a person *is* becoming rather than the arrival at a final conclusion concerning what a person *has* become. To put it another way, the good life that results from self understanding is *a work in progress.*

It may be trite to say that teaching is a very effective way of learning and that the best teacher-student interaction often results in the teacher learning more that the student. This is trite because it is true. This particular teaching experience placed me in charge of a course that took on a life of its own and I ended up learning, hopefully along with the students, a great deal.

What we learned was nothing new. The ideas expressed with respect to the evolved *teaching-learning* points of the course have been around for a very long time. The process of self discovery can only progress when a person pays close attention to experience and thoughtfully examines the impact of experience. It was Socrates who suggested thousands of years ago that the examined life is the only life worth living.[9] It was Aristotle who long ago told us that *man is a political animal*[10], that humans live in groups centered around a *polis*...institutions that tie people together in systems of social and political bonding, systems where the well being of the individual depends on the willingness to be driven by values determined by the collective.

Aristotle also suggested that human happiness results from activity that is pursued as an end in itself rather than a means to an end[11], and *there is the rub.* The group (or collective if you will) requires that system, i.e. communal, requirements be accepted by each individual as valued goals. Systems such as nations, corporations, government agencies or even athletic teams require that the individual human parts of a system pursue goals which benefit system needs such as harmony, teamwork, or profit. Individual toil, the purpose of which is the satisfaction of group values can, for the individual, be the means to midway objectives rather than ends in and of themselves. If my goal is to get along with the system and its leaders, then that goal may be a *necessary* means to accomplishing safety or security. At the same time, safety and security may not be *sufficient* to satisfy the unique yearnings of my unique self. Most inhabitants of advanced modern nations would aspire to achieving purposes that transcend bare bones survival. Most people wold not aspire to a life that does not go at all beyond the demands of the *sha na na* singers. According to Aristotle's definition of happiness, such activity— going along to get along,—may result in my safety or security but it would not result in my happiness. For most people, safety and security are means to more lofty soul satisfying ends. For most people the purpose of life is not solely safety and survival.

A philosopher of the *Enlightenment,* Rousseau[12], told us that civilization, i.e. massive social and political systems of associated mankind, can destroy the fundamental essence of the individual human. Nietzsche[13] as well suggested that the quest for equality in emerging democratic and socialistic societies would crush individual spirit and will. Freud[14] reenforced this idea by describing the psychic discontent that results from human membership in a system of civilized society.

All these diverse thinkers tell us that natural man is inherently blessed with a spirit of free will that is unique among animals and the same time he is blessed with the practical instinct of a herding creature. When these two attributes collide, however, the blessings can become a curse. Rousseau[15] advised that "Man was born free and he is everywhere in chains." As a natural organism he is free. As the unnatural part of a civilized society he is in chains.

To put it in less philosophical terms, the human condition involves potential if not the actual stress between the individual and the group of which he or she is a part, stress that comes about when one's humanity as a free spirit clashes with one's role as a member of a group, stress that can get in the way of the examination of one's life that Socrates believed was the *sine qua non* of a life well lived.

What this course did, and it was certainly not my original intention, was place these general observations concerning the *tension* between individual happiness and group demands in the context of the relationship between a complex modern organization and the individuals, the employees, who comprise the parts of an organized system. A principle take away became that road to happiness which is paved with progress toward the discovery of authentic self can be obstructed when an individual allows himself to become singularly and exclusively absorbed as an *unquestioning* part of an organized system, when a person fails to examine the consequences of his or her role as an organizational participant. The failure to examine these consequences and to react to such an examination is succinctly captured by Robert Pirsig's suggestion, in *Zen And The Art Of Motorcycle Maintenance* [16]. Pirsig invites us to explore " ...that strange separation of what man *is* from what man *does* [in order to find] some clues as to what the hell has gone wrong in this twentieth century." It seems to me, as we enter the twenty first century, that the distinction between what it means to be a human *doer* and what it means to be a human *being* is most evident when we consider the role of man as a participant in the activities of organizations.

In the chapters that follow I will examine the themes of my evolved course and delve more deeply into the nature of the life long metamorphosis of a college student into a working part of an organized system, the obstacles to happiness that may lurk in the bushes along side of the path that is trod, and the coping mechanisms that can might come in handy.

Once we accept Socrates' advice concerning the importance of living an examined life and Aristotle's notion that happiness results from activity as an end in and of itself, it becomes apparent that the key to a well lived happy life is the discovery of one's authentic self. The particular work that will satisfy us as an end rather than as a means to status or economic well being depends on the particular nature of our individuality, our soul.

The following chapters suggest answers to these questions:

- What are the obstacles to finding work as a source of happiness?
- Why does happiness depend on the discovery of our authentic self?
- How can we discover our authentic self?
- How can we determine whether or not our authentic self acts morally?

Chapter Two

Complexity of Purpose

Thus, in the shadow of organization we find all the re-
pressed opposites of rationality struggling to surface and
change the nature of rationality in practice...(T)he more
the bureaucratic form of organization advances the more
perfectly it succeeds in eliminating all human qualities ...

Gareth Morgan, Images of Organization

Ubiquitous conflict is nothing new. The Seventeenth Century philosopher Thomas Hobbes[1] observed that life is a war of all against all. Without some intrusive control of the individual, Hobbes said, "...the life of man is solitary, poor, nasty, brutish and short." Hobbes saw the powerful state as the cure for chaos. Since Hobbes' time a predominant mechanism of intrusive control that has been devised to help us progress from chaos to order is the modern organization.

Max Weber[2], the great German sociologist, discerned that modern systems of organization have one common characteristic: the bureaucratic form. Rules, standard procedures, hierarchal ladders of authority and the division of labor among specialists, comprise the basic anatomy of modern organizations, both public and private. At times, the rules are disguised as *guidelines* that allow room for desired individual creativity. Yet the demand for creativity is itself a rule. At times, hierarchy is masked. The *real* power of managers and executives is neither openly discussed nor explicitly recognized. When push comes to shove, however, the *golden rule* is that he or she who has the *gold*, i.e formal authority based on seniority, makes the rule. At times, the division of labor is camouflaged by the formation of *teams.* Nevertheless, in most modern and even in so called post-modern organizations if we peel away the structural onion sufficiently we find that some people exercise more power than others, work fits some standard prescribed pattern of decision making and behavior, and expertise varies from one individual and one group or subgroup to another. We complain about bureaucracy as a structural form of organizing. At the same time, although we would like to live without it we find that we must live with it.

The bureaucratic promise is that the mayhem of the streets will be moderated by police *departments*, international anarchy mitigated by peacekeeping military *units* under the command of national security *departments* and of the United Nations, that health will be delivered by health maintenance *organizations*, enlightenment and discovery produced by the *university*, salvation will become the yield of a *Church*, and economic security and material well being provided by the *corporation*. The very instruments that are designed to help bring all of us out of a condition of irrational chaos and into a world of rationality and order, however, are often sources of unhappiness (as well as security and survival) for many who participate in the activities of organizations.

It is virtually impossible to live in the modern world without participating in the activity of the generic organization. We depend on the vigor of organizations. We are the beneficiaries of private and public bureaucracy. We are also its victims. The life force of many people is devoted primarily, if not exclusively, to performing an organizational role. Such immersion inevitably results in the stress generated by simultaneous reward and penalty. Many find that the organizational aspect of their lives is a mixed blessing. It does not take much of an imagination to conceive of an organization that is *working*, but is not *working for you*. The Hobbesian image of a solitary, poor, nasty and brutish existence, when transposed to the context of organizational life can display an unhappy reality. Why is this so?

It is an inherent and fundamental condition of organizational life that the interests of the organization as a system and the interests of the members of the organization and the interest of the constituency of the organization, those whom the organization is designed to serve (clients and customers) are not *necessarily* the same. The idea that enables us to start to understand this condition is the notion of *purpose*.

Before we get into definitions and analysis of what is involved in unpacking the idea of purpose, let's start by looking at the story told by the film *Twelve O'clock High.*[3] Stories about military organizations are a common venue for delving into general problems created by the nature of modern organizations.The military unit is a useful analogy for any organization because organizations are potential fields of *combat.* Gordon Geko, in the movie *Wall Street*[4], is the quintessential modern executive. The *bible* that guides his organizational strategy has not to do with concepts of capitalism or management. It is *The Art of War* authored by the ancient Chinese military strategist, Sun Tsu. It is not surprising that the film *Twelve O'clock High* has been used as a case study at the U.S. Naval War College where senior naval officers study leadership and organizational problems. It should not be at all a surprise that the same film has been used at Harvard Business School where future business leaders do the same thing.

The *Twelve O'clock High* film story, which is in many respects a docudrama of historical events, takes place in the early years of U.S. involvement in World War II. U.S. leaders have decided to dedicate the Army's emerging aviation assets, organized into the form of the Army Air Corps, to the daylight precision bombing of enemy targets in Europe. In daylight, accuracy of bombing will be greater than at night. The decision to fly bombing missions in daylight, however, presents some significant problems. First of all, bombing enemy targets in daylight is a very risky business because the bombers are vulnerable to enemy ground fire and fighter attack. For this reason the British strategic doctrine calls for the "blanket" bombing of cities and enemy installations at night.

A second problem is that the U.S. is unprepared for its entry into the war. The American war machine has not yet come up to speed. There is a critical shortage of planes, in particular the B-17 Flying Fortresses that are used for the mission. There is a shortage of trained crews. In a characteristic display of self-confidence, American leaders decide to muddle through until sufficient planes can be built and sufficient crews trained.

The organization that is the focus of the story is the 918th Bomber Group. In many respect this, and groups like it, are the guinea pigs that will test the concept of daylight precision bombing and at the same time "hold the fort" until the U.S. can mobilize its manpower and industrial strength .

Based in England, the 918th consists of a number of squadrons that put up 20 or more aircraft each time headquarters calls for a bombing mission, first against German targets in France and later against targets in the German homeland itself.

The Commanding Officer of the group, Colonel Keith Davenport, has great empathy for the crews of his planes. The 918th seems to be a hard luck group, losing men and machines to enemy action at an alarming rate. The situation is particularly grim because there are no relief crews on the horizon. It is likely that the crews on scene will just keep flying until they fall victim to enemy action. "These boys can count," states Davenport. "They know they don't have a chance!"

The group is ordered to fly at lower altitudes, 9000 feet rather than the previous 19,000, to make their bombing more accurate. Davenport objects strenuously. He points out to his bosses at headquarters that the lower altitude will make his crews even more vulnerable to enemy anti-aircraft fire. When one of his navigators is chided by higher command for making costly errors, Davenport refuses to relieve the young officer of his navigation duties. It is obvious to General Pritchard, the leader of all the groups in England, that Davenport has fallen victim to "over-identification with his men" and is no longer an effective group commander. Pritchard removes Davenport from his command position and taps General Frank Savage to shape up the 918th.

Savage is a dedicated professional who sees his leadership task as taking a hard-nosed attitude. He gives the men a reality check by telling them that they "....have to fight because they are in a war, a shooting war, and some are going to have to die." He advises them that "it is okay. to be afraid" but they should "ignore that fear and consider themselves to be already dead." He challenges "anyone who is not man enough" to follow his suggestion to request a transfer from the group. The men unanimously opt for a transfer our of their flying assignments.

Aided by a loyal ground officer, Major Harvey Stoval, Savage manages to delay the written transfer requests of his aircrews. He uses the time to improve the technical skills of the crews and to develop some pride in his followers. Savage successfully solicits the cooperation of one of the youngest and most admired pilots, Lieutenant Jessie Bishop. When Bishop withdraws his request for transfer, so do the rest of the men.

Now the 918th really gets to work and starts making a useful contribution to the war effort. The odds against individual survival, however, remain high, and as Savage leads the group he loses many of his men. Although Savage does not consciously or openly admit it, these men have become his comrades in arms. He empathizes for them, but he controls his feelings because he believes the group needs a harsh task master. Savage never lets his guard down. Being the hard-nosed leader has worked for him and he continues to maintain that posture. As a result, he ends his tour as commander of the 918th with a nervous breakdown. His attempt to bottle up his feelings for his men has had a toll on his own mental stability. Savage has become a victim of the war and has learned the limits of his own humanity.

How can this story help us to understand the idea of purpose and enable us to discern a fundamental problem that can characterize life after graduation?

As we view the story, we are presented with a description of a situation, with the facts of the story. Organizations indeed are entities that can be described by facts. The job descriptions of members, the assets and liabilities, the rules and regulations, the policy and procedures, and the ladder of authority are all factual constructs.

General Savage is a stickler for the formal, fact of life, rules. When an enlisted clerk is found out of uniform he reduces him in rank from Sergeant to Private. When a senior pilot, Lieutenant Colonel Ben Gaitley, leaves the base and gets drunk during the crisis of Davenport's dismissal, Savage removes him from his position in the hierarchy and assigns him as pilot of a crew filled with misfits to fly a plane that Savage names "The Leper Colony." The structure of the organization, its anatomy is described in factual terms.

The decisions that formulate the day-to-day activity of the organization, its processes, its physiology, are based, at least in part, on factual premises. It is a fact that if the planes fly at 9000 feet of altitude they will destroy more targets than if they fly at 19,000 feet. The decision to lower the standard bombing altitude is based on this factual premise.

Organizations, however, are not just machine-like producers of action based on a factual rationality. They are also institutions, i.e. complex social systems with deeply infused values. The complex melange of values that define the essence of the organization represents a chain of means and ends that winds up identifying the highest or *end-game* objective of the organized system. It is this end-game goal that expresses the formal *purpose* of the organization. So, the formal mission, i.e. purpose, of the 918th is to help win the war. There is, however, more to it than that.

What is indeed going on is that there is more than one guiding organizational purpose, not just the one explicitly expressed by the formal mission. Purpose is the target at which all the arrows of an organization are aimed, the reason for which the organization does what it does. If a person from Mars were asked to observe organizational life and speculate on the purpose for the existence of modern organizations, the predominant social structure with which earthlings get things done, he or she (or it) would conclude that there are three purposes. Only one of the three purposes is written into policy or into the organization manual: the formally stated mission. The other two can be inferred, as would the person from Mars, by watching the behavior of the organized system and its parts.

The first, and most obvious, purpose is the formal mission, the delivery of some goods or services to a client, customer, or constituency. For the 918th Bomber Group this is helping to win the war for the American people.

Yet there are times, as we observe the way that the organizational process proceeds, as we examine the criteria that leaders and followers use for making decisions, that the purpose (end-game objective in the chain of means and ends) appears to be satisfaction of the needs of individual participants. Of course, everybody wants to win the war. As these men try to do so, however all the aircrews are going to lose their lives. It is because of this that the leader, Colonel Keith Davenport, designs the organization and runs it so that the purpose of the organization becomes crew survival.

Davenport's vehement refusal to order crews to fly at 9000 feet altititude, instead of 19,000, is a demonstration of the value premise behind Davenports behavior. Similarly, Colonel Davenport's decision to refuse to fire the weak navigator is based on the young man's very strong need to prove himself to be a loyal American even though his parents are German immigrants. The value premise of decisions made by Colonel Davenport consists of the value of preserving the lives and dignity of the aircrews. This is in conflict with the factual premise of headquarters that flying lower will result in the destruction of more targets as well as the factual premise that there are plenty of trained proficient navigators. So...we have the purpose of the organization, as expressed in the logic of the mission, in conflict with the purpose of the individual participant: to stay alive or to have his patriotism validated. If the organization is functional with respect to destroying enemy targets, it is dysfunctional with respect to preserving the lives of its members, and visa versa.

Organizations are systems of cooperation for rational action. The idea of *rational*, however, does not prescribe a specific criteria for evaluating or predicting behavior. *Rational* means the optimization of some value. I drive a large sports utility vehicle because I want to optimize the value of the capacity to tow my horses around the countryside. My wife drives a small 4 cylinder import because she wants to optimize the value of fuel economy. Both behaviors are rational because they result in an outcome that the decision maker finds useful.

General Savage wants to optimize the value of targets destroyed. That is his conception of the purpose, the end to all the means, human and mechanical, available to the 918th Bomber Group. For Savage, the death of men and the destruction of aircraft is the legitimate, even the moral, cost of doing the business of winning the war. For Colonel Davenport and for the young men who fly the aircraft of the 918th, the value to be optimized is the survival of aircrews.

Organizations do not come into existence to serve the needs of participants. It is *assumed* that the members of an organization will conceive of their own purpose to be identical to the purpose of the mission, i.e. formal purpose of the organization. That assumption is generally true, albeit an oversimplification of complex reality. The assumption is rarely true in the absolute and not necessarily true in all circumstances. Whether or not the purpose of serving the needs of members when those needs come into conflict with the formal purpose of the organization, is legitimate or is pathological, ethical, or moral, is a matter of philosophy and politics. In a socialistic system, the responsibility of institutions, both private and public, includes the nurturing of participants, perhaps to an extent above and beyond the straightforward exchange of labor for organizational benefit. Here the dominance of the purpose of the individual might not be considered as irrational or pathological. Indeed, in the early days of the birth of a welfare state in the U.S. the federal government formed organizations such as the Works Progress Administration which during the great depression in the 1930's employed millions of mostly unskilled men to construct roads, bridges and public buildings. Jobs were designed almost exclusively to serve the individual needs of the unemployed. Karl Marx's idea of a perfect society was one where the needs of each would be satisfied by the efforts of all. Where the system would be designed to serves its human parts. To the contrary, in a free market capitalistic system the benefits provided to an organization's participants are believed to be in exchange for services that accomplish a mission such as profit. Nurturing the individual just for his own sake rather than for the sake of the organizational mission would not be considered rational.When the organization is nurturing it is only because such action is considered to be in the service of the mission.

Rationality and pathology notwithstanding, even in capitalistic nations people do behave *as though* the organization *should* exist, at least in part, to serve their particular interests.

In explaining this notion to my students, I tell them that the college I work for exists, at least in part, to give me something to do when I wake up in the morning. Of course my students react to this rather glib statement by concluding that my tongue is firmly placed inside my cheek. It is not. If I believe that the relationship between me and my organization is based solely on the way in which I serve the formal mission rationality of the organization I am vulnerable to perceiving myself as a tool in the hands of another. Because the hand that holds the tool also controls the tool this might be the first step on the road giving up responsibility for my own happiness as well as a roadblock on my journey to self discovery. Philosophically, at least for me, the sanctity of the individual person,.i.e. me, the well being of my mind, body, and soul, mitigates toward giving me the benefit of the doubt when from time to time and from circumstance to circumstance I desire to use the organization to a greater extent than the organization is using me.

The question are: Am I

(a) A tool of the organization ?
    or
(b) Is the organization a tool of mine?

Of course this matter can not be conceived of as a multiple choice quiz. A more useful query would require an essay rather than the checking of boxes. Under what *circumstances* would it be beneficial for me to behave as a tool of the organization? Under what circumstance would it be detrimental for me to consider myself to be a tool of the organization? The focus of an essay that deals with these questions would be a matter of ethics or even morality. Is it ethical or moral for Savage to chide the men to "consider themselves already dead?" Is it ethical or moral for Davenport to consider that the preservation of the men's lives is of primary importance? More on this in a subsequent in chapter. For now it would be helpful to think about the possibility that the road to self discovery and concomitant happiness might be paved with the mortar of *individual* ethics and morality, i.e. on the preservation of the *self* and the purpose of *self,* rather than the unquestioning accomplishment of organizational purpose.

So...the purpose of the organization is to accomplish its formal mission. So... purpose of the organization is to satisfy the needs of its human participants.

A third purpose is the survival and health of the organization itself. One of the problems faced by the 918th Bomber Group is that the tactic of daylight precision bombing is experimental and believed by many, the British and the ground forces of the U.S.Army in particular, to be too risky and non-productive. The Army Air Corps is a relatively new organization. The willingness of American political and military leaders to devote scarce material and manpower to this organization, indeed to allow its continued existence, depends on the Corps' capacity to demonstrate that it can help win the war with daylight precision bombing. So, at times we see that the value premise of leader decisions optimizes the continued existence (survival) as an institution, and the continued resource support (health) of the Army Air Corps.

The personification of this phenomenon is the attitude of General who leads the 8th Air Force, of which the 918th bomber group is part. He tells the new leader of the 918th Group, General Savage, that his men must fly at lower altitudes and destroy more targets even though this means they may all be killed before they get relieved by other crews now in training. A sensible strategy might be to hold off and wait until they have enough crews and planes to let each crew fly a specified number of missions and then go home. This would motivate the men because they would expect the satisfaction of accomplishing a meaningful goal, the preservation of their lives. This is coming soon and this is what eventually happens. Pritchard, however, expresses his fears that if the Army Air Corps does not press on despite horrendous losses, daylight precision bombing will be discredited. That might mean the end of organizations like the 918th and perhaps of the Army Air Corps whose essence is strategic bombing. Of course, General Pritchard wants to win the war. Of course he would prefer that the aircrews survive. Nevertheless, he acts as though his highest value, his conception of the purpose of the organization is the survival and health of the 918th and the Army Air Corps even when this purpose is in conflict with the survival of the men who fly in the bombers.

In the ideal, the three purposes: mission, individual, and institutional health and survival, are not in conflict. In fact a good deal of the time the three purposes are not at all in significant conflict. Nevertheless, in the course of time, circumstances can create problems for people when leaders come to the conclusion that at this time, in this place, the interest of people needs to be sacrificed.

In this story, one of the most important functions of the leader is to integrate the divergent purposes. The new leader of the 918th, General Savage (the hero of the story), figures out a way to do this, albeit at great cost to his own mental health and at great loss of the life of the aircrews. Savage convinces the aircrews that placing bombs on target and the contribution of this to the war effort is more important to them, *as individuals*, than is their own lives. When his advice to the men to "...consider themselves already dead" results in massive resignations from a voluntary flying status, Savage zeros in on a young pilot who, by virtue of his heroism and stoicism, is respected by all air crewmen. The General tells Lieutenant Bishop that "...a *man* has to decide for himself." Bishop needs more than anything else to confirm his status as a man. To do so he must realign his values in an extreme way. He has to accept the proposition that the value of placing bombs on German targets is greater than the value of his own life. That is precisely what Bishop does. General

Savage gets Lieutenant Bishop and the others to replace their individual purpose (staying alive) with a societal purpose (winning the war). Here, the individual becomes socialized, i.e. accepts the values of the group as paramount. In all organizations, a primary function of the leader is to accomplish the socialization of followers.

The way in which General Savage convinces Lieutenant Bishop to give up his life for a cause takes advantage of Bishop's pride, his desire to be a *man*. This seems reasonable, albeit sad, to an audience which values the cause of winning the war. A cause, however, is not always universally and unambiguously admirable. In the film *Devil's Advocate* [5], the Devil in the form of the senior partner (Milton) in a law firm, takes advantage of a young lawyer's (Lomax) vanity to gain control of his soul. Both Bishop in *Twelve O'clock High* and Lomax in *Devil's Advocate* have free will. Their freedom is limited by the willingness, indeed the necessity, of the leader to push the goals of the organization against the interest of the lower level participant. Savage takes advantage of Bishop's pride. The Devil takes advantage of Lomax's vanity. "Vanity is my favorite sin," proclaims the Devil. What Bishop and Lomax have in common is that their socialization results in their destruction.

The pride of his pilots, their need to act like *real* men, is General Savage's favorite *sin*. The viewer may conclude that Savage is good and Milton, as the Devil, is evil. The form of the two stories is different, but the message is the same:

- Experiencing life as the part of an organized system means experiencing the ebbs and flows of three distinct purposes, i.e end-game objectives
  - The formal mission of the organization
  - The satisfaction of individual human needs
  - The requirement of the organization to survive and prosper
- The quintessential function of the leader is to deal with the disparity of these purposes when they come into play by making decisions that push toward the paramount objectives of accomplishment of

mission and organizational survival and prosperity. This does not mean that leaders will always have to choose between benefit to the system and benefit to the individual. It does mean, however, that circumstances can result in the individual finding himself having to cope with the primacy of organizational necessity.

Chapter Three

Natural Work

This above all: to thine own self be true Hamlet.

William Shakespeare

You, yourself, as much as anybody in the entire universe,
deserve your love and affection.

Buddha

Free will is a natural characteristic of man. This freedom is expressed in attitude, motivation, and behavior that differs from one human being to another. To put in another way, although we can assume that there is such a thing as a common human nature, it is evident that the character traits of one human being are not the same as every other human being.

In his novel *All The Pretty* Horses [1] Cormac McCarthy speculates that if we knew of the soul of one horse we would know the soul of all horses. That may be true of horses whose behavior is determined by a fright and flight instinct in the face of danger and the propensity to trust the dominant leader of a herd. Survival of an individual horse is a means to the objective of the survival of the species. The survival of the individual and the species is determined by elemental characteristics that do not conflict, that are reenforcing: individual fright and flight and the social manifestation of the herd instinct. The wild horse maintains his individuality and his devotion to group standards at the same time.

Such commonality of motivation and behavior is certainly not true of people. Even a cursory observation of human behavior results in the conclusion that a significant characteristic of human nature is the distinctive individuality of each person. Consider the difference between Colonel Davenport and General Savage in the *Twelve O'clock* story. Closer to home, consider the difference between your *self* and your brother or sister. Moreover, just as there is a difference between one person and another so there is a difference between the part of our own self that we and others can discern and the part that is concealed beneath the layers of our consciousness. Observance of self is quite different than understanding of self.

If we are to pursue the idea that the road to happiness is paved with an understanding of our *authentic* self we need to dig deeper than our personality, the behavior and attitude that we and others can observe. We need to understand the difference between what we think and do, the surface of our own humanness, our own conscious understanding of ourselves, and the inner being that is much less accessible and much more important, much more authentic. We need to understand that what it means to exist as human being can be conceived of at both a surface level and an inner level. This idea has been expressed in many ways by many different people and philosophies, all of which however, make this same point.

The most obvious sources of the duality of human nature are the world religions which recognize the human soul as the essential, the authentic, aspect of human existence. There is the body and there is the spirit.

Then we can consider what the ancient Greek Plato tells us about Socrates' conversation with his friend Meno[2]. Meno has asked Socrates if virtue can be learned. The conversation goes back and forth and in the process Socrates convinces Meno that what we think of as learned knowledge already exists inside of us, inside our souls which are provided with the eternal truth about virtue or anything else by divine powers.

Socrates demonstrates that what might be taught to a slave boy about the geometric properties of a square already exist at the deepest level, that is within the soul of the boy and all that Socrates has to do to bring this to the surface is to ask (you guessed it) Socratic questions. The ancient Greeks take on the two levels of human existence is not at all different from the take of most world religions.

The idea of surface and subsurface existence, however does not stop there. Many years after the ancient Greeks or the birth of religions Freud[3] came up with essentially the same idea, only he expressed in psychological rather than spiritual or philosophical terms. He tells us of the two levels, the conscious and the subconscious, the ego, i.e. the personality, and the super ego, the master inside of us that wants to control whatever it is we do, whatever it is we are. We could also turn to Carl Jung[4], a contemporary of Freud's who disagreed with him about many things but whose contribution to our thinking is not different from Freud's, or religion's, or Socrates' for that matter. Jung believed that all humanity was tied together by a common consciousness that is expressed in the common myths perceived by all cultures. At the same time, Jung tells us that the inner self of each individual expresses itself in the form of an archetype, a model of characteristics that expresses the authentic uniqueness of each inner self.

There is a difference between the self that we see and the self that we do not readily see. It is inherent to our existence that these two elements of our humanity can conflict. To be be happy, to be at peace, to be in a state of grace, we need to resolve that conflict.The purpose of the Catholic practice of confession is designed to do that. Sinful behavior needs be be confessed and corrected so that the soul can be soothed. Philosophic inquiry concerning the understanding of virtue is aimed at helping with that process. Knowledge of virtue needs to be teased from within the soul if we are to be virtuous. The super ego needs to be tamed if we are to be mentally healthy. The nature of our archetype has to be understood and accepted if we are to live happily with the person we really are.

Our outer self, our personality, is formed to a great extent by forces that are external to our inner spirit, our soul. The DNA which determines physical and mental attributes comes from our biological parents. Similarly, formative early childhood experience is determined by parents and others with whom we come into contact. Our educational experience molds not only our intellect, but also infuses those values that push our motivation and behavior in one direction or another. We become members of a society, we are socialized and take on the externally generated values of the social and organizational culture within which we are immersed. Prudently and practically we *get along* with what is externally imposed to go along safely and securely. To trod such a path is certainly reasonable.

Our role as parts of a system, family, nation, society, organization, civilization is not inherently pathological. It is an important aspect of life on planet earth. This idea is eloquently expressed by John Donne[5] in his poem *For Whom The Bell Tools.*

> No man is an island
> Entire of itself
> Every man is a piece of the continent
> A part of the main
> If a clod be washed away by the sea
> Europe is the less
> As well as if a promontory were
> As well as if a manor of thy friends
> Or of thine own were:
> Any man's death diminishes me
> Because I am involved in mankind
> And therefore never send to know for whom the
> bell tools;
> It tools for thee.

Indeed, no man or woman *is* an island and that fact of life is not necessarily an obstacle to a happy working life.. When, however, the forces that get us, as Donne states in his poem, *involved in mankind* —push us off the path that leads to what we desire as ends in and of themselves, our involvement in mankind in general and in the social and economic institutions of mankind in particular, can thwart the pursuit of our own interests, our own happiness.

In the *Twelve O'clock High* story the aircrews of the 918th Bomber Group accept the idea that they should succumb to the socialization dictated by General Savage as he tells them that they should "...consider themselves already dead." When General Pritchard convinces Savage that the survival of the Army Air Corps as an organization depends on proving the usefulness of daylight precision bombing and that this depends on the sacrifice of the lives of aircrews, Savage buys off on the proposition that no *clod* should be *washed away by the sea,* that no valued organization should be found to be useless. Savages' acceptance of Pritchard's leadership, however, leads to the destruction of Savage's authentic inner self. Savage's personality behavior, in Jungian terms, manifests itself as the archetype of *leader* (of a combat organization). Savage's soul, on the other hand, manifests itself as the archetype *father* (of the men he leads). Savage's physical and mental collapse at the end of the story, is the result of the the *leader* destroying the *father.* Looking at all this through the lens of Donne's poem we can see that Savage has been *diminished* by *any man's death* as he becomes *involved in mankind.* Savage is diminished by the death of his men as he becomes involved in the mankind of the men he commands.

There is a meaningful difference between what it means to be a human being and what it means to be an organization. Humans are natural organisms. Organizations are manufactured systems, man made, not natural. Organizational life is therefore complicated by the fact that natural parts function as elements of an unnatural system. Like other man made phenomena such as war, or man made institutions such as government, organizations are therefore neither inherently nor necessarily in harmony with human nature in general or with the nature of a particular person. Because of this, the achievement of happiness for the human part of an organized system depends to a great extent on human toil, as Aristotle put it, being an end in and of itself rather than *exclusively* a means to some end such as economic well being. What this means is that a happy life for most depends on a happy work experience and a happy work experience depends to a great extent on the discovery of what it is that is one's *natural work,* work that that suits your own unique nature, your own unique soul.

The idea of natural work is made clear by Herman Wouk in his novel *The Caine Mutiny*[6]. Wouk's story describes the life after graduation of Willie Keith. Willie has graduated from Princeton in the very early days of World War II. He is eligible to be drafted and both he and his dominating wealthy mother fear that he would not survive the dangers of battle he would encounter in the Army. The solution to this problem is for Willie to join the Navy, go through officer training, and spend the war as an officer aboard the seemingly safe environment of a ship.

At first Willie finds himself at Pearl Harbor waiting to join his assigned ship, the *USS Caine*. He spends his time playing the piano and singing bawdy songs at gatherings put on by the local Admiral. The Admiral offers Willie the chance to ride out the war using his musical skills as well as his charming personality in the Officers Club rather that aboard a *man of war*. A cursory bit of self examination tells Willie that such an escape from his duty as a man and as a citizen would be wrong. He rejects the Admiral's offer and sets sail on a war time adventure that will become a path to his self discovery.

Not long after he joins the *Caine* Wille receives a letter from his father. It is the content of this letter that informs us, as well as Willie, what *natural work* is and the importance of finding a life that includes such work. The letter reads as follows:

> Dear Willie,
>
> By the time you receive this letter, I think I will be dead. I'm sorry to startle you but I suppose there is no pleasant way to break such news. The trouble I've been having with my toe is due to a rather vicious disorder, malignant melanoma. The prognosis is one hundred percent bad. I've known about my condition for a long time and figured that I would

probably die this summer. But the toe began to go a bit sooner. I suppose I should be in a hospital at this moment (two nights before you leave) but I hate to spoil your departure and since there's no hope anyway, I've postponed it. I'm going to try to stall until I know you've left San Francisco. Your mother doesn't know anything yet. My guess is that I won't last more than three or four week, now.

I'm a little young to go, according to the insurance tables, and I must say I don't feel ready, but I daresay that's because I've accomplished so little. I look back on my life, Willie, and there's not much there. Your mother has been a fine wife, and I have no regrets on that score. But I seem to have led such a thoroughly second-rate life—not only compared to my father, but in view of my own capabilities. I had quite a feeing for research. When I fell in love with your mother I thought I couldn't marry her without undertaking general practice in a high-income community. It was my plan to make a pile in ten or fifteen years of such work, and then return to research. I really think I might have done something in cancer. I had a theory—a notion, you might say—nothing I could have put on paper. It needed three years of systematic investigation. Nobody has touched it to this day. I've kept up with the literature. My name might have meant as much as my father's. But now there's no time to outline the procedure. The worst of it is, now I feel your mother would have stood by me and lived modestly if I'd really insisted."

Later on in the letter, Willie's father continues:

"I know you're disappointed at having been sent to a ship like the *Caine.* Now, having seen it, you're probably disgusted. Well, remember this, you've had things your own way too long and all your immaturity is due to that. You need some stone walls to batter yourself against. I strongly suspect you'll find plenty of them there on the *Caine.* I don't envy you the experience itself, but I do envy you the strengthening you're going to derive from it. Had I had one such experience in my younger years I might not be a dying failure.

These are strong words, but I won't cross them out. They don't hurt too much and, furthermore, my hand isn't the one to cross them out any more. I'm finished now, but the last word on my life rests with you. If you turn out well, I can still claim some kind of success in the afterworld, if there is one.

About your singing versus comparative literature—you may have a different outlook once the war is over. Don't waste brain power over the far future. Concentrate on doing well now. Whatever assignment they give you on the Caine, remember that it's worthy of your best efforts. It's your way of fighting the war.

It's surprising, how little I have to say to you in these last words. I ought to fill up a dozen more sheets, and yet I feel you are pretty good at getting your way—and in other matters any words I might write would make little sense, without your own experience to fill the words with meaning. Remember this, if you can —there is nothing, nothing more precious than time. You probably feel you have a measureless supply of it, but you haven't Wasted hours destroy your life as surely at the beginning as at the end—only at the end it becomes more obvious. Use your time while you have it, Willie, in making something of yourself.....

And then Willie's father concludes with the following advice:

Money is a very pleasant thing, Willie, and I think you can trade most anything for it wisely except the work you really want to do. If you sell out your time for a comfortable life, and give up your **natural work**, I think you lose the exchange. There remains an inner uneasiness that spoils the comforts.

There is wisdom in the advice of Willie's father. First of all, he does not reject the practical matter of economic necessity nor the emotional matter of satisfying the needs of a loved one. He recognizes the requirement to deal with the present. *When I fell in love with your mother I thought I couldn't marry her without undertaking general practice in a high-income community. It was my plan to make a pile in ten or fifteen years of such work, and then return to research.* Furthermore, given the benefit of hindsight, he understands that the requirements of the present blinded him from awareness, i.e. consciousness, of his own nature and thereby prevented him from behaving in a way that was true to his authentic self. *I look back on my life, Willie, and there's not much there... I really think I might have done something in cancer. I had a theory —a notion, you might say—nothing I could have put on paper. It needed three years of systematic investigation. Nobody has touched it to this day.*

He advises Willie to focus on the present because one benefits as a result of the efforts applied to the tasks immediately at hand. *Don't waste brain power over the far future. Concentrate on doing well now.* Finally the conclusion, the teaching point if you will, is the notion that for Willie to live a life worth living he should move along the path from his present to his future consciously searching for his own unique nature and for the work that would suit that nature. *Money is a very pleasant thing, Willie, and I think you can trade most anything for it wisely except the work you really want to do. If you sell out your time for a comfortable life, and give up your **natural work**, I think you lose the exchange. There remains an inner uneasiness that spoils the comforts.*

The significance of the words that Herman Wouk puts into the mouth of Willie Keith's father has to do with more than the sad problem of *dying a failure.* The focus of his advice to his son has to do with the problem, rather, of *living a life worth living.*

The need consciously to consider the challenge of dealing with the present and keeping your focus on the search for self and for the work that is satisfying in and of itself, work that is satisfying to one's unique nature, is timeless and universal. The same problem concerning the human condition that the American Herman Wouk reveals in his 1951 novel, *The Caine Mutiny,* is expressed by the Russian Leo Tolstoy in his 1884 novel *The Death of Ivan Ilych*[7].

Ivan pursues a career in the law. He is motivated by the need for social and economic status. In time he moves from his position as a lawyer to that of magistrate and to increasingly senior and powerful positions as a judge. His marriage fluctuates from a mutually satisfying connection with his wife to periodic overt conflict. His relationship with his children is not at all gratifying. Tolstoy tells us that

> Ivan Ilych possessed this capacity to separate his real life from the official side of affairs and not mix the two...and by long practice and natural aptitude had brought it to such a pitch that sometimes, in the manner of a virtuoso, he would even allow himself to let the human and official relations mingle. He let himself do this just because he felt that he could at ay time he chose resume the strictly official attitude again and drop the human relation.... He chatted most of all about official appointments...The pleasures connected with his work were pleasures of ambition; his social pleasures were those of vanity.

As Ivan ages he becomes ill and it is clear that he is dying. Like Willie Keith's father it is only then that he becomes aware of the wretchedness of life he has lived. Indeed the emotional pain of reflecting on the path his has tread is more acute than the physical pain caused by his terminal illness. Tolstoy describes Ivan's thoughts as he confronts death.

> His marriage, a mere accident, then the disenchantment that followed it, his wife's bad breath and the sensuality and hypocrisy: then that deadly official life and those preoccupations about money, a year of it, and two, and ten, and twenty, and always the same thing. And the longer it lasted the more deadly it became. It is as if I had been going downhill while I imagined I was going up. And that is really what it was. I was going up in public opinion, but to the same extent life was ebbing away from me. And now it is all done and there is only death.... Maybe I did not live as I ought to have done...What if my whole life has really been wrong?

Both Willie's father and Ivan Ilych have become *involved in mankind,* the former as a man who needs to satisfy the material needs of his wife and the latter as a man who needs to go "up in public opinion." As Willie's father and Ivan Ilych face death, they become conscious of the fact that they have lived a life not worth living. This understanding comes when it is too late to change the sad reality. Both the twentieth century physician and the nineteenth century lawyer have accepted the role of a *resource* that can be utilized by their their profession, their organized systems, their family, and by society. The acceptance of the role of human resource blinded them during the course of their lives to the need to consider all along the importance of discovering and being true to their own authentic individuality, the reality of their own particular humanity.

Chapter Four

The Plight of the Human Resource

If you see a man approach you with the obvious intent of doing you good, you should run for your life.

Thoreau

In a real dark night of the soul it is always 3 o'clock in the morning.

F.Scott Fitzgerald

Graduation from college is a rite of passage. Up until that important day most people have been nurtured, in one way or another, by their parents, by their schools, and by society in general. The college campus, in particular, isolates students from many of the pulls and hauls of day-to- day existence. This is not to say that college students do not face problems. There is the problem of affording increasingly expensive tuition and housing. There is the emotional stress as well as the temptations of being away form home for the first time. There is the difficulty of going through the biological and behavior complications of post-adolescence. Nevertheless, the college community exists to serve the student. Teachers are engaged in the transference of knowledge that will hopefully be of some use. Counselors interact with students to advise them on their educational efforts. Administrators generate and enforce rules designed to keep students safe, to protect them from the dangers that lurk in *the outside world.* Fellow students, informally as friends and room mates, and more formally as members of campus organizations, reenforce each others need for companionship and understanding.

Before graduation parents, teachers, advisors, and friends, have had a nurturing role in a student's life. All this comes to an end on graduation day. In my more than thirty years experience as a college teacher and administrator I have have learned that the quickest way to induce panic in a Senior about to graduate is to ask the question, "What are you going to do?" The graduation day rite of passage is usually referred to as "COMMENCEMENT." What commences is the passage of the student from the relatively planned, relatively certain, and relatively nurturing environment of the campus to the relatively uncertain, relatively competitive, and relatively unsympathetic world of employment. Graduation is a door through which students pass from that stage of life where others are holding them on their shoulders to one where graduates become responsible for their own fate, their own happiness. This is a passage from the role of student to he role of employee. Whereas the role of student encompasses the dominant characteristic of *learner.* The role of employee encompasses the dominant characteristic of *human resource.*

In the past, the department of organizations which administered employee needs such as salary, benefits, contracts, promotion, and retirement, etc. was called *Personnel.* The use of the term "Personnel Department" implied the idea that employees were *people.*

In recent years the designation "Personnel Department" has been replaced with the label "Human Resource Department." Along with this change came the genesis of a nascent and rapidly growing occupation where experts might practice the profession of Human Resource Management. The change in terminology is not merely a meaningless alteration of language. The new name for the department symbolically and significantly reveals the organization's changing perception of the function of the employee. What was a human *being* is now, conceived of as a human *resource.* In this way, the usefulness of human energy and creativity that are characteristics of people has morphed into the conception of employees as matter that can be manipulated to accomplish to accomplish organizational goals.

According to the Oxford English Dictionary, the earliest use of the word, resource in 1611, referred to resource as having to do with finding a new source water. The expression *human resource* melds the notion of human with that of an inert material.The implication of the new term is that organizations can elicit the life force of human beings in the same way that material resources are drawn from the generosity of nature. However, the attributes of nature with respect to natural materials such as water, or metals, or wood, are different from, and in some respects contradictory to, the fundamental qualities of human beings: individuality, soul, self, free will. The process of managing people involves the attempt to accomplish mission objectives and system well being. When human beings are perceived of as human resources, a managerial attempt will be made to mold, socialize, and manipulate people in the same way that inert materials are shaped to produce a product. The not so tender trap for people, then, is the temptation, indeed the apparent rationality, to put aside a self conception as human being and to accept the self conception as human resource. That is exactly what happened to Doctor Keith in *The Caine Mutiny* story[1], to Ivan Ilych in Tolstoy's novel[2], and to the aircrews in the *Twelve O'clock High film*[3].

Closely related to the conception of people as human resource is the striving for efficiency and this term is similarly problematic. The word and the concept of efficiency has traveled from the realm of engineering to the realm of organizations.

Organizations are systems of cooperation for a purpose. As an organization strives to accomplish its mission, inputs of human energy, material, and fiscal resources are to be converted into outputs that will accomplish the purpose for which the organization was created. This process is influenced by a utilitarian ideology the core of which is the necessity to control the relationship between the cost of inputs and the quantity of outputs. More production (output) per aggregate of cost (input) results in greater efficiency. Less production per aggregate of cost results in less efficiency. Profit, for example, is an indication of the relationship between cost (input) and revenue (output). The word profit is a synonym for efficiency, intrinsic to the language of efficiency. The same can be said of the expression cost-effectiveness that is so common in public or non-profit organizations.

The use of the language of efficiency is not original to organizations. It has been transported as a metaphor from domains that have nothing at to do with organizational matters. According to the Oxford English Dictionary, the original meaning of the term efficiency is "The ratio of useful work performed to the total energy expended or heat taken in." Originally the notion of efficiency dealt with the operation of engines. An engine is a mechanical contrivance for transforming energy by means of the periodical repetition of a cycle. The efficiency of an engine is the proportion which the energy is transformed to a useful form. More friction internal to the engine, more energy wasted and less efficiency of engine operation.

Just as the term human resource has traveled from the realm of nature to that of organizations, so the term efficiency travels from the realm of engineering to that of organizations. In a profit making organization the input-output metric that has jumped from the field of engineering is expressed in monetary terms that are unambiguously commensurable. If the formal purpose (mission) is profit and the output is cars manufactured and sold, the extent to which the mission has been accomplished can be discerned by calculating the difference between revenue and costs. In a nonprofit or public organization the bottom line efficiency metric is expressed in terms of cost-effectiveness.

The need to understand the use of the expressions *resource* and *efficiency* goes beyond the mere play of words per se. Language and the images that language evokes, reflect thinking and influence behavior. The way we think, what we experience, and the meaning of what we do every day is very much a matter of the language that we use. The exercise of leadership is not necessarily driven by explicitly understood and articulated factors. Quite to the contrary, behavior is often pushed by the images aroused by language in a manner that is not obvious to the practitioner.

Language can become the driving force of organizational action. This is particularly true when contingencies are too complex or too dynamic to be handled sensibly by any particular clearly specified strategic theory. Indeed, the chaos of the post modern environment can overwhelm the straight forward linear strategic behavior. As it becomes more and more demanding for people to make sense of a complex and at times chaotic and unpredictable organizational environment, language becomes more and more a powerful instructive phenomenon, more and more of a path to understanding and even effecting attitude and behavior. As George Orwell explained so vividly in his novel *1984*[4] the control of language results in the control of people.

When an organization's culture is driven by the language of *human resource* and *efficiency* leaders may perceive subordinates as passive tools to be manipulated. Charlie Chaplain's film *Modern Times*[5], previously mentioned, displays a satirical image of human beings used as human resources to effect efficient production. Here, the leader is motivated to focus on employees as tools to be used in the service of an organization and to ignore the authentic selves, the humanity, of the humans they manage.

At the start of this chapter the point was made that in the early stages of an individual's education, that is life before graduation, the student is likely to be the beneficiary of a good deal of nurturing, of catering to the deeper aspect of an individual's humanity. As one enters life after graduation, as one enters the world of the *human resource* and the world of *efficiency,* catering to the yearnings of the one's inner self, one's soul if you will, is less likely. This is why the road to happiness that one may travel after college is marked with warning signs that reveal obstacles to discovering one's authentic self and responding to the urgings of that self. The capacity to attain a state of happiness depends on the ability to read these signs and the will to obey their message.

Chapter Five

The Professional vs.
The Manger

*People seem not to see that their opinion of the world is
also a confession of character*

Ralph Waldo Emerson The Conduct of Life

The following relevant film scenarios clarify the logic of the human resource and efficiency metaphors as well as demonstrate the consequence of the potential robustness of the human sprit. Films stories can inspire those facing life after graduation to look for hero role models whose outlook and behavior suggest a path to a fulfilling life. Stories can also show us villains whose behavior should not be imitated.

In this chapter the film *Network*[1] shows us how the perception of human beings as human resources and the quest for organizational efficiency can result in control of human activity from the top of a hierarchy and tragic consequences.

In the chapter that follows this one we will see that the film *Rollerball*[2] suggests that heroic, one might even say courageous, individual values and behavior can result in the triumph of a morality that is pulled from the bottom up, a morality that gauges the expenditure of the life force of a human being as a critical cost and the goal of satisfying human aspirations as an essential goal.

Let's start with *Network.* In this film story we observe an organiza-tional sea where the fish swim in currents and counter currents of om-nipresent conflicting values and interests. The text of *Network*, the story that it tells, is a compelling criticism of the way that television displaces individuality and freedom with an overpowering mass culture. The perpe-trator of wrongdoing is the *tube* and the victim is the passive audience that accepts what comes over the *tube* as truth. On the other hand, the context of the story, its circumstance, reveals the culprit to be the orga-nizations that produce and deliver television programs. In the situations described the organizational system villain is the network and the human villains are the network's corporate masters.

The victims are the professional journalists who have the job of deliv-ering the revelations of a false god, TV, to attract, even seduce, viewers. The tragic mechanism is the ratings system and the quest for economic efficiency by way of audience approval that results in profit derived from selling commercial time.

At the professional level we have the News Division of UBS Network. The News Division is unique. It is not a profit center. Other divisions of UBS Network report to the network leadership. The News Division re-ports directly to corporate headquarters (UBS Systems). Other divisions, such as the Programming Division, are considered to be profit centers and are held responsible by UBS network executives for the ratings that result in profit (or loss) by way of selling advertising. The News Division is free of this constraint. The delivery of news is considered, at least at the start of the story, to be a pubic service, distinct from the over all profit mission of the organization. This arrangement is gratifying to the professional journalists who derive satisfaction from providing a service to society in general (as compared to service to the organization *per se).*

The central characters who inhabit the News Division are two ac-complished middle-aged professionals. Max Schumaker leads the divi-sion. Howard Beale is the evening news anchorman. Max and Howard are longtime friends who entered their profession at the earliest, and for them the happiest, days of television news broadcasting. The arrangements that enable the News Division to operate independent of a profit motive are well suited to both Max and Howard's professional ethics. Of course, Max and Howard's substantial salaries satisfy pragmatic needs. Delivering truth in the form of news to the public, however, is the paramount objective of professional journalists. Such a goal is an end in and of itself, a goal that, at least according to Aristotle, the attainment of which results in happiness. Here at the professional level of the organization, Howard and Max pursue their natural work, work that that fulfills the aspirations of their authentic selves.

The Programming Division of the network *does* report to network executives and is responsible for the production of the high audience viewer ratings that result in profit. Programming is under the direction of the Vice President for Programming, Diana Christensen, a young, attractive, upwardly mobile, ambitious, even ruthless, manager. She craves the pursuit of ratings and profit.

Diana is not at all pleased with the status of the News Division. She yearns for profit over public service. She is motivated to accomplish the profit mission of the organization as well as to increase the survivability and health of the organization. These two purposes conflict with the purpose of providing a news service to the public and a home for the professional journalists, such as Howard and Max.

The UBS network is under the control of UBS Systems, a large communication corporation that owns a wide variety of media subsidiaries operating in TV, radio, magazines, etc. This corporation is under the direction of Frank Hackett. Hackett has become increasingly involved in the detailed operations of UBS.

UBS Systems is acquired by CCA(Communications Corporation of America) which is in turn absorbed by WWF (World Wide Funding), a holding company of global dimensions. The Chairman of WWF is the executive, Mr. Jensen.

A clash of purposes exists from bottom to top. Howard and Max (in the News Division) are motivated to inform the audience of the truth. This is the purpose of their profession and the source of their job satisfaction.

Here the metaphor human resource is not valid. Howard and Max are much more than material to be manipulated by the corporation. Neither is the idea of economic efficiency valid. Max and Howard implicitly perceive of a metric of accomplishment in terms of an input of journalistic labor based on the expertise of the journalist and an output of truth that is displayed on nightly TV news programs.

Contrasted to this, the managers, Diana and Hackett, are motivated to maximize profit by maintaining a high level of program ratings. They perceive people, especially the news professionals Howard and Max, as resources to be utilized in the service of profit.

At the top of the corporate hierarchy Mr. Jensen is driven by an ideology that advocates the globalization of business. This has nothing to do with either the profits desired by Hackett and Diana or truth telling that is the professional function of Max and Howard. Jensen sees the purpose of the organizations he commands as proselytizing the formation and perpetuation of a global economy where political, economic, and social power resides in the hands of corporations and their captains. Jensen's focus is on the external environment. He relishes a future where corporations evolve to be the masters of the world by way of control of the global economy. His emphasis is on the purpose of optimizing the health, one might even say the dominance, of the corporation as the driving force in world affairs.

At the different levels of the corporate structure we see the professional journalistic truth telling purpose pursued in particular by Max and Howard, the managerial purpose of profit, pursued by Diana and Hackett, and the strategic motivation of Jensen to bring about a world where the corporation per se dominates all matters of human existence. As the story unwinds we see that the three purposes conflict as well as the consequences to human beings who are conceived of as human resources.

At the start of the story Howard Beale is a mandarin of TV. His fortunes, however, both personal and professional, are on the decline. His wife has died, his youth has faded, and the ratings of his show are declining. He is morose. He drinks heavily. As a result of poor audience ratings,

Howard is fired by Hackett who has managed to make the News Division responsible for ratings. Hackett considers Howard to be an expendable resource.

As the network ratings plummet, Diana and Hackett decide to put Howard back on the air, not as a newsman but as a commentator who may attract audiences as he rants and raves denouncing the hypocrisy of our time. Howard decides to accept Hackett's offer. By doing so he becomes a willing pawn in the power game, a resource to be used in the service of ratings and therefore profit.

Howard Beale goes on TV with the comment, "I must make my witness." He announces that "Everybody knows things are bad. The dollar buys a nickel's worth. Punks are running wild in the streets. The air is unfit to breath. The world we're living in is growing smaller. I want you to get mad. You have got to say —I am a human being, my life has value— I want all of you to get up right now and go to the window and yell, I'm mad as hell and I'm not going to take this any more—"

People all over the country do exactly as Howard asks. When Diana hears of this she says, "Sonofa bitch, we struck the mother lode!" The Howard Beale show becomes the top ratings show in news and the fourth best in all TV. At a meeting of network affiliate stations Diana gives a triumphant speech. She is now famous as the woman behind the highly rated Howard Beale show.

Howard quenches the flaming ambition of Diana and Hackett. He informs his audience on live TV that Western World Funding Corporation (WWF), with Jensen at the helm, is buying CCA for somebody else, the Arabs. Mr. Jensen becomes upset when Howard rages on, telling how the Arabs are buying up the U.S. Howard publicly criticizes the CCA deal because foreign ownership of American assets is ruining the American economy. He tells his audience to telegram the White House and say, "I'm as mad as hell and I'm not going to take it anymore. I want the CCA deal stopped now."

Howard is upsetting the apple cart of Mr.Jensen, the head of WWF and its subsidiary CCA. CCA has indeed borrowed $2 billion from the

Saudi's. Jensen has arranged for this debt to be settled as the Arab nation comes to own CCA. With Saudi ownership of an American communications corporation, the global economy will be one step closer to achieving Jensen's dream of a brave new globalized world were corporations replace nations as the dominant players in the game of world affairs.

Jensen wants to use Howard to preach his ideology of corporate domination on the air. He calls Howard to the WWF boardroom for a face-to-face confrontation. He forcefully lectures Howard.

> You have meddled with the primal forces of nature and I wont have it. The Arabs have taken billions and now they must put it back... There are no nations, no peoples, there is only one holistic system of systems...multinational dominion of dollars... petrodollars, marks, francs, shekels, yen...It is the international system of currency that determines the natural order of things on this planet today. And you have meddle with the primal forces of nature. And you will atone! There is no America, no democracy, only IBM, ITT, Union Carbide, Exxon etc. Those are the nations today. The world is a college of corporations determined by the immutable bylaws of business. The world is a business. It has been since man crawled out of the slime. Our children will live to see that perfect world in which there is no war or famine, oppression or brutality, one vast and ecumenical holding company where all work to share common profit, all necessities provided, all boredom amused. And I have chosen you to preach this.

When Howard asks, "Why me?" Mr. Jensen replies, "Because you're on TV, dummy."

Now the network is presented with a severe problem. Mr. Jensen wants to keep Howard Beale on the air. He wants Howard to preach the ideology he has so forcefully explained. He wants to use the network for propaganda rather than profit, to use the network as a tool to control the global economy and to use Howard as a tool, i.e. resource, to control the programming of the network.

Howard accepts the role of human resource. When his News Division colleagues chide him he replies with "That's my job you are messing with." Howard's quest for security overcomes his pursuit of truth telling as an end in and of itself. Howard is falling off the path that will guide him to a life worth living, or indeed any life at all.

On live TV Howard tells his viewers that democracy is a dying giant and that individual freedom is finished. That is exactly the message that Mr. Jensen wants him to deliver. Howard's new theme is that dehumanization might not be so bad after all. This is a depressing argument. Nobody wants to hear that his life is valueless and the ratings of the show dip significantly. With low ratings, the power position of Diana and Hackett becomes fragile. The pursuit of profit is threatened. Diana needs to fire Howard to improve the ratings. At the same time Hackett knows that Mr. Jensen has taken a strong personal interest in the Beale show. If Howard stays on the air, UBS and CCA profits will decline. Hackett, the manager, however, cannot fire Howard, the professional, because Howard has the support of the executive at the top. Mr. Jensen thinks Beale delivers an important message. He does not care if the Beale show loses money and he will not allow Beale to be fired.

The notion of economic efficiency, i.e. the optimization of revenue per unit of cost, i.e. profit, which is the quintessential goal at the managerial level, has clashed with the quest for achieving globalization at the executive level. Howard Beale, who has forfeited his role as a professional journalist, has become the human resource caught between the proverbial rock and a hard place.

Hackett, Diana, and other UBS and CCA managers meet and decide that the only solution to their problem is to assassinate Howard Beale. Diana believes that if they get rid of Howard, they can recover ratings. Short of that, UBS stands to lose $45 million in advertising revenue because of the poor ratings of the Beale show. Hackett agrees. He tells the assembled executives, "I suppose we'll have to kill him." Diana arranges for a gang of hit men to do it live on the show. Howard Beale is assassinated on the air.

The movie ends with a comment from an unseen narrator: "Thus Howard was the first man who was killed because he had lousy ratings."

This story shows us how the quest to achieve the purpose of mission, in this case profit, by managers, can overcome the prospect of conceiving of Howard Beale, the professional, as a human being, rather than simply a tool to achieve an organizational goal. Similarly, the desire of Mr. Jensen to use Howard to advocate an ideology of corporate globalism, even at the sacrifice of profit, and eventually at the sacrifice of Howard's life, demonstrates how executives can use up a human being just as they might use up fiscal or material resources.

One way of attempting to avoid the harmful impact of being used as a resource to accomplish efficiency is to concentrate on assuming a role as a professional. As an individual becomes increasingly focused on a singular function based on specialized expertise, values based on service to society in general or to a particular client, and a code of behavior shared with other experts, he assumes the role of professional. This is the role assumed by Max in the *Network* story. Max leaves the organization as a result of the destruction of the professional function of the News Division. For Max, professional responsibility transcends responsibility to an employer.

Specialized training and socialization as a professional seems like an attractive way to define ourselves, to conceive of our work as an end in of itself rather than a means to an end. The physician may enjoy reaping the economic benefits of his work. The essence of the purpose of his labor as a professional, however, is healing as an end in and of itself. Certainly, Max saw his role as a professional journalist. His purpose is informing the public and this comes into conflict with Diana and Hackett's purpose of achieving the ratings that would result in profit.

Practicing as a professional would be a handy way to move toward acting in accord with our authentic self. The problem, however, is that the professional working in an organizational setting often bumps up against leaders, managers, and executives who play roles that are made up of values which conflict with those of the professional. Because of this, maintaining the integrity of the professional role can become problematical.

Professional expertise and values can be the basis of a well integrated persona for the individual and the foundation for harmony among colleagues. Often such harmony is threatened by inherent conflict between managers and professionals. The process which determines the outcome of such conflict is a matter of organizational politics. The relationship between managers and professionals is inherently a political relationship.

A useful definition of politics has been suggested by David Easton.[3] He defines politics as the authoritative allocation of values. The dominant value of the manager, indeed what the manager is attempting to manage, is the optimization of efficiency. Resources are always scarce and therefore they must be husbanded in order to accomplish organizational purpose. The central identity of the manager is *optimizer of resource use.* The source of the authority of a manager is position power, power derived from the manager's senior position at the more lofty rungs of the organizational structure.

On the other hand, the dominant value of the professional is to bring specialized expertise to the table to produce a desired effect. The central identity of the professional is *application of expertise.* The authority of the professional is the power of expertise. The manager, no matter how much efficiency is achieved, cannot accomplish organizational purpose, without relying on the expertise of the professional. The relationship between the manager and the professional is therefore a political relationship. The outcome of this relationship is determined by which values are "allocated" i.e. implemented. In the tragic *Network* story those are the values of the manager.

The way in which these two roles can conflict and the way that the conflict may be resolved as a result of the process of organizational politics is dramatically revealed by the tale based on actual events told by the film *The Right Stuff.*[4] This film chronicles the adventures of the original seven Project Mercury astronauts, the first Americans in space. The true to life story demonstrates the way that professionals can develop political strategies to maintain the integrity of their profession and the endurance of their identify.

Because the job description "astronaut" had not previously existed, seven men were chosen from the occupation that seemed most closely to resemble the emerging profession of astronaut. They were all military test pilots. As test pilots, the seven men shared the expertise of flying experimental aircraft to the limits of designed performance envelopes and beyond. They shared the ego satisfaction of the daredevil. They shared the discretionary power granted to them by nurturing military organizations which were dependent upon them to maintain United States dominance in military aviation. They shared the isolation from management provided by the secrecy of their tasks, the esoteric nature of their duties, the high risks inherent to their mission, and the unpredictability of their airborne experimentation.

The film introduces us to the test pilot as a free spirit. This role is personified by the quintessential of all test pilots, Chuck Yeager. When we look at his life style, we see a picture of a man who is much more in touch with *himself* and his *compatriots* than his bureaucratic organization, the Air Force.

As military test pilots, these men were not at all in conflict with their organization. They were isolated from the organization, practicing as individual artists responding to the whim of their authentic selves soul rather than to the dictates of managers. Savage and the 918th Bomber Group, in *Twelve O'clock High,* may have been flying in accordance with the orders of General Pritchard. These test pilots, however, were used to flying by the seat of their *own* pants.

The competition for assignment to the civilian agency, NASA, and for the designation *astronaut* is intense. Only those who have the right stuff will be selected. What, however, is exactly, is the right stuff? Is the stuff it takes to make an astronaut different from the stuff it takes to make a test pilot?

The seven men who are selected to be astronauts believe that the transition from military test pilot to astronaut involves only an upgrade in status. They seek this recognition and see their new profession as no different from the old one. Significantly, Chuck Yeager chooses not to compete for the astronaut job, but rather to remain in his military test pilot role. Yeager realizes that the transition to astronaut will involve more than just a change in uniform and title.

As newly minted astronauts, the seven men become part of a highly politicized, highly bureaucratized, agency— NASA. The U.S. is losing a race with the Soviets who have already placed an orbiting manned satellite into space. The technology is speculative. Development of the project is in the hands of NASA bureaucrat-managers allied with rocket scientists who have been imported from post-World War II Germany. The politics of the space program are driven by the President's promise to put an American on the Moon within ten years.

NASA accepts the astronauts into the agency not as independent practitioners of an esoteric and heroic profession, but as tools in a complex organizational machine designed to accomplish the space mission quickly and efficiently. The problem for the astronauts is that the experiment of probing space does not necessarily require the placing a man in a space capsule. There is no doubt that the technology exists to navigate in space by remote control. A human being need not be in the cockpit to control the craft. Indeed the earliest space probes were occupied by a chimpanzee. If there is human presence, the requirement for life support systems and the use of over-engineering to provide for safety grossly complicates the technical problem of space exploration. From the perspective of the scientists and engineers designing the Mercury spacecraft, and from the perspective of those managing the project, the man/pilot is redundant, if not useless. Because of this Chuck Yeager has referred to the astronauts not as brave and skillful pilots controlling the course and the fate of their craft and but as "spam in the can!" having been put in the capsule for the political purpose of beating the Soviets in the race to put a man on the moon.

As the training of the seven astronauts and design of the Mercury capsule nears the completion the seven men are shocked to see that the prototype capsule has no window. The addition of a window would weaken the structural integrity of the craft and increase the cost of producing a workable space capsule. Managers are keeping their eye on the criteria of efficiency. From the managerial perspective, the window is an unnecessary cost that produces no useful effect. NASA can get a man into space efficiently even if he cannot see where he is are going.

Yeager, it seems, was right. The seven men realize that without a window in the space capsule they are going to be "spam in the can" after all, just along for the ride.

The unhappy professional-astronaut-specialist now has come into severe conflict with his organization. Six of the seven men have no idea how to deal with this conflict. The seventh, John Glenn, has the right stuff in a way that was not anticipated. Glenn believes that a man in the capsule is necessary because only the presence of the human expert will be able to deal with all the unanticipated contingencies that space exploration will involve. Glen believes that the role of astronaut and the role of test pilot are the same. Program managers, on the other hand, believe that standard procedures and automation can handle the mission and that the man is redundant, along for the ride, along to satisfy the President's political a promise of outdoing the Soviets.

The right stuff that Glenn is made of is the stuff of organizational politics. He understands that support for the expensive project depends on public opinion. Public support, Glenn realizes, depends on the heroic image of the astronaut and on the long range goal of putting a man, not a monkey, on the moon. Glen sees that politics at the national level can trump the quest for managerial cost-effectiveness at the organizational (NASA) level.

Glenn takes charge of the situation and solves his colleagues' problem by informing NASA administrators that without a window the seven men will withdraw from the project. If this happens, he informs his seniors, there is no pilot for the craft and without a pilot there are no heroes, and without heroes there will be no public support, and without public support there will be no funding authorized by Congress. "No Buck Rogers," Glenn tells the project managers, "No bucks." The managers of the project realize that Glenn is right, that Glenn has more power that would be revealed by the organizational chart. They order the construction of a window.

In this story once again we see the juxtaposition of the role of the professional and the manager. The result is the process of organizational politics. We observe the battle between those who see the practice of their profession as an end in itself (in this case the test pilots) and those who assume the role of manger.

The occurrence of this sort of conflict is inevitable because at the core of the manager's ethic is the requirement for efficiency, the careful husbanding of resources. For the manager, the scarcity of resources is an all-important fact of life. For the professional, the core ethic is the requirement to apply specialized expertise to get the job done. The limiting resource, for him, is neither material nor fiscal. What matters is skill and the self-confidence to apply that skill. Because the application of professional skill most often takes place in an environment of uncertainty, the professional practitioner desires slack resources, i.e. more to work with than is prescribed by the necessarily parsimonious calculations of the manager. In this case, the demand for a capsule window is not merely the result of the ego of the test pilot. The requirement is also a result of the test pilot's knowledge that the aerospace domain is fraught with uncertainty and that the human mind is the best tool for dealing with surprises.

The story of the astronauts and the space capsule window is a lucid indication of the peril of unhappiness faced by all professionals employed by modern organizations. The universality of this situation is so apparent that it borders on the trite. What physician does not feel frustrated by the hospital manager's desire to keep costs down by, for example, limiting the number of tests conducted in a diagnosis procedure? What professor is not perplexed by the Dean's push to increase efficiency by mandating higher average class size? What engineer is not irritated by a project manager's concern with limiting the quality of materials used or restraining the engineer's desire to "over engineer"? What police professional is not frustrated by administrators and politicians who restrain his use of force to apprehend criminals?

When I make the point to my students that there is inherent conflict between the manager's concern with efficiency and the professional's concern with producing a desired effect, I throw seven or eight pieces of chalk out of the window. I tell them that the managers (we call them administrators) of the college would be upset with me for doing this because the act is a waste of resource and, after all, the budget is not unlimited, even for the purchase of such mundane items as chalk. On the other hand, because I obviously care about the effective transfer of abstract knowledge from myself to my students more than I care about the chalk bill for the administration, I desire to conform to professional values.

In *The Right Stuff* and in *Network* we see a demonstration of the manner that professionals come into conflict with managers. Now let's take a look at another potential source of unhappiness, another potential obstacle to practicing one's natural work. This is the conflict between the professional and the society that he or she seeks to serve.

Neither the professional nor the organization that employs him function in a vacuum. The organization and its experts exist to serve society in general and the organization and the expert practitioner depend on the support of society. Private organizations continue to exist only as long as clients, constituents, or customers, demand particular goods and services. Public organizations exist only with the blessing and the funding of governments. (Remember: "No Buck Rogers, no bucks.")

The individual, the organization, and the society are connected by mechanisms of control. Rules of the game, either explicit or implicit, are established. These are designed to affect the behavior of the expert and produce results that are predictable and acceptable. Mechanisms of control are put into place to thwart what has been called the *tyranny of expertise*[5]. The physician is told to refrain from the use of medicines that are not approved by the Food and Drug Administration, even when in his professional judgment it might be rational to use unproven experimental drugs. The engineer must build to the specifications of a governmentally sanctioned code. The scientist must conform to rules concerning the use of human subjects in experiments. The teacher of young children must eschew corporal punishment, even when the expert teacher knows that a slap on the fanny might be a valuable contribution to the education of the child. What is valuable the the eye of the professional can be tyrannical in the eyes of society.

As experts become narrowly focused on their own competence and as they strive to accomplish a professional purpose, it is plausible, we might say inevitable, that they come to believe that they know what is good for society to a greater extent than the members of society know. This belief is a source of unhappiness for the expert practitioner who wants to put his specialized competence to use at his own discretion, who wants to be fully engaged in his natural work, without societal constraint. I tell my students that I am a professional and that I direct all my efforts to serving them. They come back with the argument that if I exist to serve them then why do I work them so hard? Why do I hold their feet to the fire? Why do I grade them by using high standards? My retort is that they *hire* me because I know what is best for them better than they themselves know. At times, I wonder if this manifestation of my desire to practice without the assessment of my students is indeed tyrannical.

The stereotypical tough detective portrayed in the film *Dirty Harry*[6] believes that the legal and social constraints of due process are to be avoided for the benefit of society. He plays by his own rules. Dirty Harry may be very good at catching and punishing criminals, but in the end he suffers at the hands of those who would control his behavior. In the film *High Noon*[7] the sheriff rejects the pleas of citizens that the town should avoid a risky confrontation with criminal sociopaths. The hero sheriff is determined to save the town in spite of itself. The citizens of the town want all people, including the sherif, to ease off and opt for personal safety. Even though he saves the day when he guns down the bad guys and marries the beautiful school teacher, the sheriff experiences profound sadness and disillusionment. He is hurt by the fact that he has to disobey the townspeople in order to help the townspeople. The architect in the film *The Fountainhead*[8] sees himself as a singular repository of excellence and taste. When he disapproves of the design of a publicly approved and funded housing project, he destroys the buildings by committing a criminal act of arson. He believes that his professional standards are more worthy than the standards of the people who will live in the buildings. His professional standards, however, are the *fountainhead* of his own agony.

Society demands, and even craves, the skill of the expert and is often accepting of the narrow view that accompanies such skill. If I have to undergo brain surgery, I do not care if the surgeon understands and is compassionate with the holistic nature of my situation or my humanity. I just want someone who knows exactly how to perform brain surgery. I want brain surgery to be his natural work. If I am the passenger on an airliner, I do not care whether or not the pilot accepts the precepts of Judeo-Christian ethics or the ideals of liberal democracy. I just want a pilot who knows how to get me to my destination in one piece. I want to be informed by an expert journalist and I want that information to be objective and in full detail. Yet it will upset me very much if I perceive that: the brain surgeon sees me as a piece of meat to be carved with precision, the pilot is not sympathetic to the vulnerability I feel as we hit a thunderstorm, the broadcaster refuses to cater to my desire to be entertained as well as informed.

The expert who is practicing his natural work is confronted with the ironic problem of his own expertise. He is squeezed between the rock of his expertise and the hard place of the holistic needs of those he serves as well as the control impulse of the manager. The motivation to go on to graduate school and pursue life as a professional (engineer, scholar, lawyer, scientist, physician, or whatever) is inviting. It is reasonable to assume that the acquisition of expertise that is in demand will result in economic security, job satisfaction, and the reward of sharing values with fellow professionals. To pursue one's natural work as a professional, however, it will be necessary at times to deal with, as did John Glen, the power of managers as they strive to restrict the application of expertise. To pursue natural work happily, a person must also adapt to the way that society restricts the unrestrained practice of professional expertise as it did in the *High Noon* and the *Fountainhead* stories.

Chapter Six

An Heroic Pursuit of Natural Work

It matters not how strait the gate
How charged with punishments the scroll,
I am the master of my fate:
I am the captain of my soul

W.E . Henley

We have seen that the invidious impact of the human resource metaphor persists when the quest to achieve managerial or executive purpose is pushed from the top down. The insight and imagination of the following story suggests, however, that heroic, one might even say courageous, individual behavior can result in the thwarting of top down power and the triumph of the human spirit.

The film *Rollerball*[1] describes a world where nations are no longer the basic political and economic unit of humankind. A rearrangement of the players on the worldwide stage is the result of disastrous world wars caused by the inherent instability of a global structure which consists of conventional nation states. Reorganization of the global structure has been based on corporations replacing nations. (Think about the ideology of Mr. Jensen in *Network*.)

A world structure based on many corporations is, however, considered to be too fragmented. Competition among corporations looks uncomfortably like tribal warfare. Accordingly, the fragmented pieces are integrated into functional Divisions: Transport, Food, Finance, Communications, Energy, and Housing. The executive leaders of these six Corporate Divisions make up a Board of Directors that controls world affairs. Six executives make all decisions, ostensibly for the common good. Each functional Division has its corporate headquarters in an urban center: Energy in Houston, Food in Chicago, Communications in Tokyo etc.

Now everyone is comfortable. All material needs are provided. This is what the executive Jensen, in the *Network* story, was hoping for. Beyond the basic needs, there are many luxuries available to all. The Corporate System takes care of everyone. All the Board of Directors ask is that people do not question or interfere with executive decisions.

Dysfunctional competition among the mega-units (Energy, Communication, etc.) and the resultant aggressiveness of the units themselves are resolved by channeling competitiveness into the domain of sports. The sport of Rollerball has become the substitute for all forms of harmful competition, including war.

A Rollerball field of play is laid out inside a massive arena located in each city that hosts a corporate Division. A slick oval banked surface provides a track around which the players, some on roller skates, some on small motorcycles, can circle at great speed. The action starts when an official launches a heavy mellon sized ball onto the floor of the track. The object of the game is for a player to pick up the ball and sink it into a pipe that is the trackside goal. Skating players use the hitch-handle on the back of teammates' cycles to speed up their progress around the track. As opposing team members attempt to gain control of the ball and sink it in the pipe, the action is fast and furious and loaded with violence.

Defending against a player headed for the goal often requires striking the skating or cycling opponent and doing great bodily harm. The violence on the track is reflected in the excited attitude of the fans. Fan loyalty goes beyond the ordinary identification with a team. It springs from a deep sense of patriotism and chauvinism – devotion to a cause.

The Rollerball season ends when the best teams compete for the world championship. The defending champion this year is Houston.

Rollerball players occupy a unique place in society. They are a combination of Knights in Shining Armor and Gladiators. They represent the marshal spirit. They protect the honor of their cities. They also provide an outlet for the aggressive disposition of the citizenry.

Skating for the Houston team is Jonathan E. Jonathan is the best Rollerball player in the world, a hero of heroes. He has had a long and distinguished career. Rollerball is his natural work. Rollerball is his life and a good life it seems to be. His comfort and security needs are catered to in the extreme. Jonathan lives in the lap of luxury. He is adored and admired by all, including the series of young and beautiful women that, at the direction of the Houston executive hierarchy, have shared his ranch-mansion since the mysterious departure of his wife.

Houston is nearing its goal of a championship season. First they have to beat Tokyo and then New York.

Mr. Bartholomew is the Executive Director of the Houston Corporation. His most important human resource is Jonathan. Bartholomew is having a hard time thinking up rewards that will continue to motivate Jonathan. Jonathan has everything he needs. Bartholomew does not understand, or take into account, that the most important reward for Jonathan is the life affirming satisfaction of participating in the game he loves, sharing activity with his colleagues, and winning for the Houston fans. Jonathan as a champion Rollerball player is the quintessential example of a man engaged in his natural work. For him the game is an end in itself itself and not a means to an end of fan adoration or corporation provided luxury.

Bartholomew decides to put on a special *multivision* show that will tell Jonathan's heroic story. This, he believes, will stroke Jonathan's ego. There is more, however, to Jonathan's situation than the need for ego stroking. He is told that there are corporate Directors who want him out of the game. Jonathan has had ten glorious years. He is perceived by the Directors to be a threat because he commands dedicated unquestioning fan loyalty. Some of the executives want the special *multivision* program planned by Bartholomew to be used to announce Jonathan's retirement. An old friend tells Jonathan, "They are afraid of you, all the way to the top they are." The Directors fear that the fulfillment of Jonathan's human needs to excel at the game and his popularity with the Houston fans will result in his achieving power that may overwhelm the capacity of executives to control the global economic and political environment.

Mr. Bartholomew tells Jonathan that "No player is greater than the game itself. It is not a game a man is supposed to grow strong in." Clearly, Jonathan is considered to be a human resource.

Jonathan's life energy is totally devoted to his role as a player in the game. He desires neither more fame, nor fortune, nor power. He points out to Mr. Bartholomew that the team depends on him. Bartholomew tells him that the game serves a social purpose as a substitute for aggressive competitiveness and that this is more important than the needs of Jonathan which are fulfilled by his participation as a player. Bartholomew fails to appreciate Jonathan's point of view and tells him that if he does not retire willingly, he will be forced into retirement.

Now the Houston team faces Tokyo. The Board of Directors has decided that in this game there will be no penalties and only limited substitution for injured players. The rules have been changed to make the game more violent, more interesting to the crowd and more dangerous and threatening to Jonathan.

Bartholomew tells Jonathan that he is to retire, not to play against Tokyo or ever again. Jonathan rebels and the Houston executive is embarrassed when Jonathan fails to announce his retirement. Subsequently, Jonathan is told that if he retires, his future comfort is assured. The Houston Energy Corporation will treat him well. Jonathan, however, wants more than ever to play. He defies the powers that be and plays in the Tokyo game. Jonathan rejects the role of human resource. He acts to satisfy the needs that drive him from within. It is the value of winning as a result of human expertise, and his loyalty to team mates and fans that propels Jonathan's rebellious behavior.

The Tokyo game turns into a melee and Jonathan's best friend is so severely injured that he is pronounced brain dead. Jonathan mauls an opposing player and then scores the winning goal. The crowd goes wild. Houston will play NewYork for the world championship.

Before the championship game a management problem has to be solved. The Board of Directors, consisting of the leaders of each Corporation, are in conflict with Bartholomew. He has lost control of Jonathan. This creates an intolerable situation for the Houston executive. Bartholomew agrees that Jonathan is an obstacle to world stability. He proposes that in the next game there will be no rules, no substitutions for injured players, and no time limit. The game will be played in conditions of anarchy. Given Jonathan's drive to win, he will probably sacrifice his life for the good of the team. There will be no accidents, nothing suspicious. "Let the game do its work," Bartholomew tells his fellow executives. "The game," Bartholomew points out, "was created to demonstrate the futility of the individual. If the champion defeats the meaning for which the game is designed, then he must lose."

Jonathan's rejection of the role of human resource is in conflict with Bartholomew's desire for power. The Director-Executives vote to go ahead with Bartholomew's plan of an anarchic game, a plan designed to bring about the demise of Jonathan.

We witness the championship game, Houston vs. New York. We wonder, if there is no limit on the time played, how can you have a winner? The answer is that that they will play until all players die, including Jonathan. Thus, the executive plan to do away with a recalcitrant planer will be successful.

The violence begins. A player is thrown into the blood thirsty crowd and beaten. Jonathan continues to play effectively despite being assaulted by others. The crowd turns against him and chants, "Jonathan is dead!" The Houston coach tells his players "This was not meant to be a game...never."

Neither team has scored. There are injured and dead players spread over the field of play. Jonathan is on the track faced by two remaining opponents, one on a motorcycle and one on skates. Jonathan breaks the neck of the New York skater right in front of Bartholomew. The cyclist goes after Jonathan. It is now one-on-one, *mano-a-mano*. Jonathan has the New York player down and can kill him by bashing him with ball. The crowd is silent. Jonathan takes off his helmet. He stares at Bartholomew. He places the ball in the goal. Houston has won the world championship. The crowd chants, "Jonathan!!! Jonathan!!!" The hero circles the arena. He is in his glory.

The courageous spirit and the strong will of Jonathan has enabled him to reject the role of human resource. He has thwarted the executive quest for using him as their tool. Jonathan devotes his life force to the achievement of his own aspirations. He pursues his natural work even at great risk. He has achieved a state of happiness.

In both stories, *Network* and *Rollerball,* the organization pursues the goals consistent with the purpose of mission and the preservation of economic health and survival of the organized system. The managers of the TV network, Hackett and Diana, strive for the ratings that accomplish profit and this will result in the continuing existence and growth of the organization. To accomplish goals they treat Howard Beale as though he were a human resource and when that resource, in the hands of Jensen, thwarts their desires they kill Howard. The corporate executives in *Rollerball* similarly conceive of Jonathan as a human resource. Their political and economic strategic purposes require the maintenance of power at the top. This comes into conflict with Jonathan's purpose, the pursuit of his natural work.

Of course, the purpose of the individual worker is neither necessarily nor consistently in conflict with the purposes of the organized system. Yet harmony between the system and its human parts is not guaranteed and at times can be fragile. In both these cases there comes a time and a circumstance when push comes to shove, when the human *being* experiences the unenviable metamorphosis to status as a human *resource.* In the Network story the circumstance involves conflict between various layers of the complex corporate hierarchy matrix, between the holding company (WWF) lead by Mr Jensen and the network (UBS) lead by Hackett. In the Rollerball story the circumstance involves conflict between the mega-system of globalized corporations and the aspirations of the individual. The possibilities for conflict are limited only by the imagination.

What should be considered as one contemplates a working life is that, as Mr. Bartholomew points out, the organizational *game* can be manipulated to "demonstrate the futility of the individual." The outcome depends to a great extent on the ability of the individual to understand his or her authentic self and the capacity, indeed the willingness, to maintain the integrity of that self. Howard Beale fails the test and Jonathan gets an A+.

Chapter Seven

Workers Paradise... or Not?

Do not do unto others as you would that they should do unto you. Their tastes may not be the same,

Shaw

The film stories told in the previous chapter suggest that organizational life at times is experienced in conditions that demonstrate the futility of the individual. The conventional wisdom tells us that this may be true at some times, in some places, and in come circumstances, but it is certainly not always true.

If we wanted to take an optimistic view or life after graduation we might look with envy to the people who work at the *workers paradises* that function in Silicon Valley, California where high tech corporations seem to treat hight tech employees in a way that gives very high priority to the happiness of workers. Google Inc., for example, proclaims to its employees that

> Our benefits exist to make sure that you are well taken care of. Your family matters to you, so they're important to us, too. We have a number of benefit programs and on-site amenities to support you and your loved ones through

life's various stages and situations. Hey, we are family...
When it comes to our benefits and perks, we have everything you'd expect from a large company, like health
insurance, retirement benefits and so on. But we also offer way more than the basics. Our benefits are part of who
we are, and they're designed to take care of the whole you
and keep you healthy, whether physically, emotionally, fi-
nancially or socially.... Googlers solve complex problems
everyday in the name of our core mission to organize the
world's information and make it universally accessible to
our users. But what makes working at Google truly unique
is the workplace culture that encourages innovation and a
healthy disregard for the impossible.[1]

The facility occupied by Apple Inc. in Silicon Valley provides a working environment that looks and feels more like a vacation property than a factory. Picnic grounds, a gym, and a company store provide a paradise-like
environment. Luxury buses transport employees back and forth between
Cupertino and as far away as San Francisco. A new Apple Campus with an
covers 176 acres of scenic lands planted with apple, cherry, apricot, plum,
and olive trees. Employees have access to a fitness center complete with
a basketball and volleyball gymnasium, group exercise facilities, physical
therapy space, a cafe, and a training staff to manage fitness and recre-
ational activity. Apple employees rave about the great food at Caffe Mac
located in Apple's main headquarters in Cupertino. So far so good.

As the brave new world of high tech progress evolves, however, the
value of technically qualified people increases and the demands for
skilled tech workers starts to outpace the supply. As the competitive
nature of the tech business increases workers can demand increasingly
impressive salaries by making their services available to any firm that is
willing to bear the load. No longer are employees willing to spend the
entire lifetime of their careers working for one firm. As a result, the profit
and future development of high tech firms comes into conflict with the

purpose of qualified employees to optimize their economic welfare by hiring out to the highest bidder.

In addition, the outsourcing of work, particularly to China, becomes increasingly attractive because the cost of labor overseas is considerably lower than in the heady atmosphere of Cupertino and its environs. Significantly, the demand for luxurious working conditions, the realistic aspiration to work in a workers paradise, does not exist overseas. Firms like Apple can function in places like China in a way that profit trumps working conditions and workers economic aspirations.

So...what happens when push comes to shove? What happens when workers in the U.S. working for firm A see an opportunity to earn more money at firm B and firm B takes action to snatch firm A's human resources?

In April of 2014 Dan Levine of Reuters news reported[2] that four major tech companies including Apple and Google agreed to pay a total of $324 million to settle a lawsuit accusing them of conspiring to hold down salaries in Silicon Valley by preventing one company from hiring the employees of another. Tech workers had filed a class action lawsuit alleging corporations schemed to refrain from soliciting one another's employees in order to avert a salary war.

The case was based largely on emails in which Apple's late co-founder Steve Jobs, former Google CEO Eric Schmidt, and some of their Silicon Valley rivals hatched plans to avoid poaching each other's prized engineers.

In addition Apple, Google, Adobe and Intel settled a U.S. Department of Justice probe by agreeing not to enter into no-hire deals in the future. The four companies had been fighting a civil antitrust class action.

Although the organizational ship sails through smooth water most of the time, stormy weather is at times somewhere on the horizon. Agam Shah of IDG news[3] service reported on September 2, 2014 that Apple Inc. was under fire again for the way workers were treated at a supplier factory in China, prompting the iPhone maker to rush a team to investigate. A report by China Labor Watch and Green America revealed forced overtime, fire safety risks, poor compensation, and exposure to toxic chemicals a factory in China at factories operated be Apple supplier Catcher Technology. [3]

Occasions of worker mistreatment is not limited to overseas operations. On November Nov. 13, 1974, union activist and plutonium plant worker Karen Silkwood was found dead in what police ruled a single-car accident. The circumstances, however, surrounding her death have kept people guessing to this day.[4]

Karen had worked at a $4 per hour job as a metallography technician at the Cimarron plutonium plant operated by Kerr-McGee near Crescent, Oklahoma. Her duties there included polishing fuel rods packed with radioactive plutonium pellets. While at the plant, she joined the Oil, Chemical & Atomic Workers Union, which staged a strike at Cimarron not long after she started working there. When the strike ended in failure, many of the workers severed ties with the union. Silkwood, however, who as a member of the bargaining committee (the first woman to hold the position in the union's history) was charged with investigating health and safety issues at the plant. In the summer of 1974, Silkwood testified to the Atomic Energy Commission that she had found serious violations of health and safety regulations including evidence of spills, leaks, faulty fuel rods and enough missing plutonium to make multiple nuclear weapons. She also alleged the company had falsified inspection records.

On Nov. 5, 1974, during a routine check, Silkwood discovered she had been exposed to over 400 times the legal limit for plutonium. She was sent home with a sample kit to conduct more self-tests. The following morning, despite having handled no dangerous materials as part of her job that day, she tested positive once more. On Nov. 7, plutonium contamination was found in her lungs and she was sent to Los Alamos National Laboratory in New Mexico for further testing. Silkwood believed she was deliberately contaminated as a result of her whistleblowing efforts against Kerr-McGee.

By Nov. 13, she had decided to go public with her story. She gathered evidence documenting the plant's wrongdoing and was on her way to meet a national representative of her union and a New York Times reporter in Oklahoma City when her car went off the road and struck a culvert, killing Silkwood. She was 28.

Silkwood's father and children filed suit against the company, not for wrongful death, i.e. having Karen run off the road and therefore murdered, but for willful negligence leading to her plutonium contamination. The family's lawyers were harassed, intimidated and even physically assault-ed. The jury, nonetheless, found in their favor, awarding the family $10.5 million. On appeal, the amount was reduced to a mere $5,000 – to cover the destruction of Karen's personal belongings during the decontamina-tion of her apartment. The U.S. Supreme Court reversed the case and it was headed for retrial when Kerr-McGee settled out of court for $1.38 million. They admitted no wrongdoing as part of the settlement. [5]

The study of the functioning of modern organizations, mostly in the realm of social relations and social psychology, tells us much, but does not predict with accuracy whether organizational life will be friendly to the pursuit of individual happiness or destructive of human aspirations.

The first attempt at increasing the efficiency of business organiza-tions came about early in the 20th Century. The ideas captured by the term *scientific management* came about as the results of the efforts of Frederick Taylor, the very first management consultant.[6] Taylor be-lieved that there is one best way to accomplish any given task. He and his followers set out to explore and implement that notion by conduct-ing time and motion experiments that would reveal paths to optimal ef-ficiency. *Scientific management* and its related theoretical offsprings came to be known as *theory x.*[7] *Theory x* and its many variations either explicitly or implicitly considers the working person to be a tool of the organization and the function of the manager to be the devising the one best way, the most efficient way, to utilize the human resource. Henry Ford's use of a production line assembly process to manufac-ture his early model automobiles is an example of the manager putting *theory x* to practical use.

A dramatic critique of *theory x* is the film *Modern Times*[8] staring Charlie Chaplain. The film opens with a mob of workers approaching a factory to get on with their jobs. Human workers are portrayed as herds of crowded sheep blindly following a leader to they know not where.

Inside the factory we see Chaplain, as the poor soul on the assembly line repeating and repeating the same standardized use of a wrench to tighten bolts as they pass by. Chaplain's efforts and those of his fellow *sheep-workers* are observed by the factory manager who uses a pre-modern version of a security camera to look at and evaluate factory floor operations. The manager is not satisfied with the speed of production and orders a muscular naked-to-the waist sweating foreman to pull levers that will speed up the assembly line. As the line speeds up, Chaplain and his fellows must speed up the repetition of their singular contributions to the manufacturing process. As he uses his wrench over and over with increasing speed, Chaplain's whole body vibrates to the frequency of his use of the tool. In fact, his whole personae has become a tool of the manager. Having lost control of his body, Chaplain falls onto the moving belt and is thrust into the large gears of the factory machinery. He goes round and round meshing with the finished product.

The attempt of high tech firms to prevent one another from hiring tech experts who might want to move to another company and glean higher wagers is behavior consistent with the general thrust of *theory x*. So is the use of Chinese labor by the suppliers of high tech firms.

The ideas of Taylor were challenged, starting in the 1920's by a group of Harvard professors lead by Elton Mayo[9]. These fellows working at a Western Electric plant started out with the notion that improved working conditions would increase production efficiency. The initial results were mixed. It was expected that increased lighting at individual work stations would increase productivity and that decreased lighting would decrease productivity. These hypotheses were in accord with the notions of *Scientific Management*. A little *grease* applied to the (human) instrument and it might function more efficiently. Increased lighting it seemed would be one element of the one best way to get things done. Observed data, however, demonstrated that in a significant number of cases both increased lighting and decreased lighting speeded up production.

Subsequent interviews of the workers observed resulted in Mayo and his colleagues concluding that workers became motivated to increase productivity because they perceived, having experienced being observed by the fellows from Harvard presumably with clip board and stop watches in hand, that management perhaps for the first time was showing a real interest in the day-to-day, hour-to-hour experience of the workers. The presence of the experimenters led workers to perceive that they were part of the same social system as their managers.

Subsequent experimental observations of groups working together to accomplish the wiring of electrical banks resulted in further conclusions which contradicted the fundamental premises of *theory x*. Data from these observations led to the conclusion that the working behavior of the groups was determined by group norms, informal rules about rate of work, when to start, when to stop, when to take breaks etc. rather than formal rules that management has specified to accomplish productivity. In other words, the productive behavior of individuals that were part of a working groups was determined by the social relations among members of the group. It was in this way that it came to pass that the newly proposed *theory y*[10] spawned the social relations movement. The fundamental idea was that the managers should conceive of their organizations as social systems where the accomplishment of results, the fulfillment of the systemic purposes of the organization, would depend on the cognitive and emotional attitude of workers as they perceived themselves as human parts of a social system joined in the harmonious pursuit of common ideals and objectives.

The workers paradise environment established by firms like Google and Apple, as well as their generous benefits packages and perks like luxury bus transportation are consistent with the thrust of *theory y*. So is the statement in Google's human resource literature which proclaims that

> Our benefits exist to make sure that you are well taken care of. Your family matters to you, so they're important to us too.

In this way an attempt is made to encourage workers to see themselves as pursuing their natural work, to conceive of their organization as a social system, one big happy family, rather than a machine that grinds out product solely for the purposes of profit and institutional vigor.

Closely related to fundamental assumptions of *theory y* is *theory z* formulated by Willaim Ouchi[11] and often called "Japanese Management" relating to the style popularized during the Asian economic boom of the1980's. *Theory z* focuses on increasing employee loyalty to a company by providing a job for life with a strong focus on the well-being of the employee, both on and off the job.

What is the significance of all this theory generation and management behavior to a person considering, indeed living, life at work after college? The take away point is that in over one hundred years of theory development and practice the *fundamental* premises of both *theory x* and *theory y* persist. The good news is that life after graduation can offer the opportunity to pursue one's natural work in the nurturing environment of what is in effect a social system such as the one specified in the Google human resource literature. The bad news is that there is always the *possibility* that the luxury bus ride, the gym, the friendly cafe, will morph into the *Rollerball* game with no penalties and no time limits experienced by Jonathan E, the death by hit squad experienced by Howard Beale in the film *Network*, the radiation poisoning experienced by Karen Silkwood, the feeding machine experienced by Charlie Chaplain, and the attempt to have their freedom to move to another firm blocked by high tech worker firms.

It is tempting to conclude that Chaplain's film portrayal of the factory manager using a camera system to observe, evaluate, and ultimately control worker production is out of date. It might also seem reasonable to view as no longer relevant Henry Ford famously pacing his factory floor with a stopwatch, timing his workers activity in a bid for greater efficiency and hiring private investigators to spy on employees home lives to make sure personal problems did not get in the way of worker performance.[12] Modern Human Resource managers as well as most up to date organization theory literature would tell us that *theory x* is dead, having been replace by more sophisticated management strategies. The practices characterized by Taylor's notion of *Scientific Management,* however, are far from extinct.

In 2009 UPS (United Parcel Service) fitted its delivery trucks with about 200 sensors that track everything from driving speeds to stops for the driver to rest. In this way managers find out which drivers were taking unauthorized breaks. In this way the maximum possible number of deliveries could be squeezed into one day.

A computer attached to a McDonald's cash register has been used to capture how well a server sells customers on the latest deal offered by the company. In some supermarkets computer generated information can record how quickly a cashier scans each grocery item sold. In this way management can determine how hard each employee is working and how necessary each employee is to the business[13].

In the next chapter the persistence of seemingly conflicting theories and practices that affect the environment of the working world will be examined as well as the way we can make sense of a working mileu where the pulls and hauls of contrasting management strategy results in apparent chaos.

Chapter Eight

Making Sense

Man is what he believes,

Chekhov

Both *theory x* and *theory y* over the years have spawned a strain of related ideas and practices. As we look at the artful fiction that tells us about the meaning of the working lives of people and as we examine factual accounts of reality we can see that one paradigm or strain of ideas and practice has not replaced the other.

A plurality of leadership strategy continues to influence the way that one might experience life after graduation. We can understand the way that knowledge accumulates and is put into practice by considering the notions of the philosopher of science Samuel Kuhn. Kuhn explained in his 1962 book *The Structure of Scientific Knowledge*[1] that fundamental ideas that deal with absolute truth, he called them paradigms, shift from one era to another. The conventional wisdom suggested Kuhn, was that as time goes on progress is made and one paradigm may replace another. Ptolomy's idea that the sun revolves around the earth was replaced, for example, with Copernicus' and Galilleo's proof that it was the earth that revolved around the sun.

Kuhn challenged the conventional wisdom by proposing that scientific truth, at any given moment, cannot be established solely by objective criteria, but is defined by a consensus of a scientific community. Since consensus is not always complete, rather than one paradigm necessarily replacing another competing set of ideas, both can be accepted and put into practice at the same time. Competing paradigms, according to Kuhn, are frequently incommensurable, that is they are competing and irreconcilable accounts of reality. One set of ideas is comparable to apples and the other to oranges. Apples and oranges may be considered both to be fruit, but you cannot add 5 oranges to 5 apples and get 10 apples. Furthermore, if rival theories cannot be directly compared, we cannot make a rational choice as to which one is better. In the final analysis, which one is better may depend on the details of circumstance, the situation, the phenomenon to be considered, rather than on one all encompassing theory that explains everything. At least that is what Kuhn thought.

A frequently cited field of science that at least hints at the validity of Kuhn's thinking is physics. Classic physics, the physics of Isaac Newton, consists of a set of ideas, a paradigm, that explains the nature of matter and energy on a scale familiar to human experience, including the behavior of astronomical bodies. The impact of the force of gravity of the planets and the sun of our solar system, for example, enables us to predict the exact position of the moon at any point in time. Certainly, this knowledge enabled man to find the moon and to go to the moon. Similarly, the idea that every action has an equal and opposite reaction is the basis for the function of the rockets that propelled man to the moon. The classic physics of Newton is still relevant.

Toward the end of the 19th century, however, scientists discovered phenomena in both the large and the small systems of matter and energy that classical physics could not explain. Thus arose the physics paradigms based on Einstein's theory of time, i.e relativity, as well as the theories of quantum mechanics that deal with matter and energy by considering the very smallest elements of matter which behave in ways that cannot be explained by classical or Newtonian physics. The physics of the smallest pieces of matter has not replaced the physics the the larger lumps. The two paradigms, as Kuhn suggested, are incommensurable.

Similarly, the paradigm of organization theory that explains worker behavior and prescribes management strategy that sprung from the head of Frederick Taylor, and the ideas that were first suggest by the Hawthorne Western Electric plant experiments conducted by Harvard professors exist side by side. There is no overarching grand theory of organizational life or organizational effectiveness. If there were, then graduate schools of business such as at the prestigious school Harvard, would teach that theory to business leaders of the future and expect them to put that theory into practice in the same way that students in medical schools learn about various ideas that explain the pathology of the human body. The process of management graduate education, however, rather than relying on putting theory into practice mainly uses the study of analysis of detailed case studies. Since one case is different from another, the emerging manager learns how to deal with a wide range of distinct contingencies rather than how to apply a singular set of ideas. In other words the answer to the "how to" questions of management (so called) science has to start with the words "it depends." The process of management decision making and strategy formulation that does have an impact on the quality of the life of the people they manage involves a search for the answer to the question "On what does it depend?"

A working life then cannot be understood by way of comprehending any single formula results in happiness. If there were a singular set of ideas that dominated the way that the working world works, life after graduation might be predictable or at least easy to understand. It is neither.

The process of living an examined life, the road to the understanding of self, and the quest to practice one's natural work, involves the attempt to make sense out of a seemingly senseless working world, a world where many paradigms compete in a wide variety of circumstance.

The point has been made that there is no overarching grand theory that can guide us to work that fits our individual natural self, work that we can pursue as an end in and of itself. Because of this, the future that may lead to happiness as we pursue a life after graduation has to be planned in a way that accounts for our own unique reaction to our own unique experience, and our own unique inner self.

The only person who can discover our authentic self is our self. This cannot be done by sitting back, thinking carefully, and coming up with an all-inclusive, complete, thorough, comprehensive strategic plan and then just implementing it. Of course this would be the most stress free way of marching bravely into the days and years to come. That's what all of us would like. Yet we instinctively know that this cannot be done and that is the reason that the worst possible question one can ask a graduating senior is "What are you going to do ....now?" We would like to use reason to set our sights on a happy future by thinking deductively, by acting according a generalized notion of how we should set our sights. Yet since you are not a generic human entering a generic world this is not doable. The process of making sense is one that at best can evolve over time incrementally rather than comprehensively. This is especially true as the modern world slips not so gently into what some people refer to as post modern, a world where chaos rather than order seems to be the nature of the life we enter after graduation. There is no school catalogue now. There is no student handbook. There are no specific graduation requirements. There are no syllabi. There are no professors to tell what to do and how to do it. There are no midterms. There is no final exam. There is not even a grade!

As we march from the past into the present and the future the more complicated the problem of pursuing happiness becomes. Once upon a time there were kings and nobles and serfs. Everyone knew who they were, what they were supposed to do, the role they were to assume. These traditional roles were dots of status conferred by birth. The dots were connected by the economic, military, and charismatic power of kings and queens, power used to maintain the status quo. The picture formed by the connected dots was sometimes pretty and sometimes ugly. A theory of divine right explained the picture as well as motivated people to conform to the might of the explanation. Once upon a time everything made sense.

Eventually, the picture was blown apart by the winds of modernity: political revolution, religious reforms that spawned the Protestant work ethic, industrialization, and capitalism. When the dust settled, the new dots were the well-defined roles assumed by politicians, administrators, managers, financiers, scientists, and engineers. The dots were connected by a rational system of organization called bureaucracy, a system that promised efficiency, a structure specified by hierarchy, rules, and division of labor. The picture formed by these connected dots was sometimes rewarding and sometimes disappointing. A theory of *scientific management* explained the picture as well as motivated people to conform to the might of the explanation. Everything made sense.

Now, the well-defined and static picture of modernity is being squeezed out, destabilized by post-modernity: a revolution in the acquisition, computation, arrangement, and transmission of information (computers); a virtual universe that exists side-by-side with the natural cosmos (cyberspace); the harnessing of the atom for good and for evil; the obscuring of national boundaries by a process of globalism, terrorism, environmentalism and immigration; technical progress that puts great power in the hands of experts of both the good and the evil variety; the demand for services that overshadows the demand for goods.

Now, the dots themselves, the roles that people play, are stressed by the centrifugal force of individualism and the centripetal power of community, the pull of self-interest and the push of empathy, the quest for privacy and the demand for exposure.

In the workplace, the legitimacy of hierarchy is called into question by the moral imperative of equality and the dependence of politicians and managers on professionals. The efficacy of division of labor is mitigated by the increasing need for teamwork and interdisciplinary skill. The usefulness of rules is mistrusted as standardization becomes a less reliable method of using complex means to accomplish elusive goals. The connecting of dots has become problematic. Now, the dots themselves are not well defined. This is a crisis of individual identity where the discovery of self becomes increasingly difficult as the criteria for identifying clear cut roles to play becomes increasingly fuzzy.

Moreover, as the world has changed, the traditional and modern methods of connecting the dots, of making sense, have not atrophied. The traditional status structure fathered by the gods of power and wealth remains. *Scientific Management* has not disappeared. An attempt to discover, and to put into operation, the one best way is still with us. The promise of efficiency made by organizing work in the framework of a bureaucracy is still seductive, even in our so-called post-structural era. The old theories of traditional divine right, management that attempts to find the one best way, and bureaucracy have been augmented, but not replaced, by new ideas, such as those that suggest that rationality is bounded, that organized systems are open to complex external environments, that decision-making is incremental rather than strategic, that interdependence of units of work is pervasive and complex.

One method of understanding the world of organization and living in that world has not replaced another. The lines that have the potential for connecting the dots, for making sense, are like the blooming of a thousand flowers. The world in general—and the world of work, in particular—is characterized by complexity and ambiguity. Nothing makes sense.

To function, however, participants in the everyday world of work need to make sense, or at least try. When objective reality is unclear, it is reasonable to expect that a subjective social construction of reality will take place in an attempt to untangle a snarl of complexity. When our thinking results in the confusion and discomfort of ambiguity and dissonance, it is reasonable to expect that perception will be modified to create a more comfortable image, one in which the dots can be connected. The reasonableness of these ploys of connecting the fuzzy dots, of coping with the postmodern world of work, is explored by an emerging set of ideas called *sensemaking* [2].

At the heart of the sensemaking is the idea that people make *retrospective* sense of their present circumstance. They form a picture of past experience and push it through a lens that filters out the chaos and confusion of absolute reality so as to form i.e. construct, an image that makes sense. What one experiences is captured by a framework that can encompass the complex occurrences of the future, that can explain surprises, contain them so that they might make sense, a framework that can help one understand what to expect when predictions based on so called objective analysis break down. A person *reads* what has happened in the past so that he or she can author, i.e. control, what happens in the future without being bogged down by the confounding confusion of new and surprising experiences.[3]

The complexity of life as a freshman, for example, can be frightening and usually is. The stressful experience of freshman year, according to the idea of sensemaking, results in each individual creating a mental frame of reference in which to place the zigs and zigs and the surprises which will be experienced during the on going college years. As time goes on the student replaces the fog and the complication of actual reality with a social, i.e. mental, construction of reality that makes sense. The reality that the freshman actually confronts is confounded by confusion: What courses do I need to take? What should be my major? What do I do about this loneliness that I feel? How can I complete this paper when I have midterms to study for? Where is the money for my tuition going to come from? By the time these details are coped with the senior confronts the same actuality he did as a freshman, but he makes sense out of his situation by creating, i.e. authoring, a manufactured reality that is much more sensible:

The difficulty of any course is determined by the grading standards and attitude of the professor and I can find out about this by keeping my ear to the drumbeats in the dorm; I can do the paper by carefully checking the internet and then doing an all nighter; somehow the tuition problem will take care of itself; loneliness is gone because I have a great social life; nobody ever failed out of this place.... and more. The senior's absolute reality is in fact not much different from that of the freshman. The mental and emotional picture that the senior has of reality, one that enables him to cope with the real complexity and the real surprises of his real situation, however, is much more friendly, much more sensible.

As a college professor I would much rather teach freshmen than seniors. The freshmen have to deal with the reality that I present them with and therefore it is possible for me to manage them, to motivate them, to control their attitude and behavior. When it comes to the seniors they have created their own reality. They are much less confused, much less malleable, and therefore much less manageable. At the same time the sensemaking that makes controlling classroom outcomes more difficult for me, the more experienced student is one step closer to acting out the scenario of his or her own individuality. If that individuality thirsts for learning, my efforts are effective and my job satisfaction is high. If that individuality rejects a search for knowledge my efforts are thwarted and my frustration swells.

As students we experience the stresses and strains of higher education. Yet as alumni we go to reunions and to sporting events with a very rosy picture in our heads of our days on campus. What we have done is place the seemingly senseless complexity and complications, the stresses and strains of our years in college, into a frame of reference that makes sense. We have socially constructed reality.

My own years as a student at the rigorously disciplined environment of the U.S. Naval Academy at Annapolis, Maryland consisted of survival based on the promise of the arrival of graduation day and a resultant escape from strict hierarchical day-to- day control. The same might be said, to a greater or lesser degree of my classmates. Yet now, many years later, when we gather at reunions or join in groups to joyfully cheer on the Navy football team, we reflect on our days on the shores of the Severn River as the happiest days of our lives. For many of us this happy state is the result of sensmaking which created a frame of mind that empowered us to pursue a career that offered an experience of natural work. Those who did not find a career as a Navy or Marine Corps natural or successful simply do not attend reunions.

The same might be true in the working world in general. As workers over time start to make sense out of the complex and not always comfortable working world they tend to march to the beat of their own drummer rather than the beat of mangers and executives. Perhaps this is why the highly qualified high tech workers in Silicon Valley sued their employers who were attempting to restrict their vocational mobility. The sense these workers made was placed into a frame of reference that told them that loyalty of their present employer did not make them happy and that it might make sense to search for greener fields.

Of course, making sense of a situation does not in and of itself guarantee getting closer to being in touch with our authentic self. Yet as we reflect on our experience (i.e. in accordance with Socrates admonition to live an examined life) and think about our reaction to the chaos that is so prevalent in the post modern world, we can come closer to understanding way in which our choice of work affects our happiness or lack thereof.

The following chapter will make the point that stories which explore the complications and the problems of organizational life, can help us to make sense out of the complexity and complications we can expect to experience as we pursue a working life after graduation. Sensemaking theory tells us that the reality we construct as we move along through the years helps us to cope, helps us to maintain the integrity of our own individuality, helps us to discover our authentic selves. Stories, even fictional stories, that we can explore in the here and now can provide us with images and imaginative insights that can serve as surrogates, or at least hints, of the actual experiences that we might encounter in the future.

Chapter Nine

Stories as Surrogate Experience

Where there is leisure for fiction there is little grief,

Dr. Johnson

When I sat down to lunch with three friends I had not seen for some time, I expected the conversation to be technical and professional. It was our working lives that had brought us together in the past. Now we were meeting as old friends, a sort of reunion. All of us are experienced professionals: two professors and two retired naval officers. Our common working interest and expertise is the study of modern organizations in general and specifically the vulnerability of some organizations to serious, costly, irreversible errors (plane crashes, collisions at sea, nuclear meltdowns, etc.).

As long-time practitioners, as well as students, of the art of organizational life, we had plenty of "data" to chew over. Our experience was theoretical and bookish as well as empirical and real world. We did not have to ask superficial questions to start a conversation, questions like "Have you seen any good movies lately?" Yet the first words uttered were, "Have you seen the movie *Titanic* ?" From there the conversation turned to the proposition that if the ship had not been turned in a vain attempt to avoid the iceberg, she would have hit it straight on and would not have been fatally damaged. Then we went on to discuss other movies that vibrated sympathetically with our interest in error and disaster: *China Syndrome... Doctor Strangelove ....Towering Inferno.....*

It seemed odd that we who considered ourselves to be practitioners of social science as well as thoroughly modern, if not scientific, managers and leaders, wanted to focus our attention on fiction, the movies; but maybe this was not so very odd. Fiction, after all, can be a powerful source of truth, the sort of truth that cannot be revealed by mere facts, the sort of truth that divulges the *meaning* of what it is we experience and observe, what it is we are, what it takes to make us happy, or miserable, the sort of truth that can lead us to making sense of organizational life.

Later, when I thought about the lunch and the conversation that centered on disaster movies, I thought that we had avoided discussing what might be the most persistent disaster of all: the day to day internal battles that go on between organizations and the individuals that are the parts that make up the whole organized system: organizational members. I thought about the stresses of organizational life. The tension between individual and communal needs is one problem that has always been part of civilized human experience. The individual needs the group and the group needs the individual. Yet the group can get in the way of individuality. Membership in an organizational community that becomes an obstacle to happiness is a specific case of this universal human predicament.

Social scientists and the managers and executives who put the principles proposed by the social scientist to use see organizational life predominately through the lens of the organized system. Does the artist, the teller of stories, have a different perspective? If so, what is the perspective of the artist? Can the perspective of the artist help us to make sense of what our working lives after graduation may look like?

No scholar sums up the usefulness of fiction to help us make sense of organizational life better than Barbara Czarniawska-Joerges. She tells us that a work of art can be very personal in tone but still have an objective quality. This aesthetic quality, which some people might want to call 'truth' is not subjective or arbitrary. It has an objective relevance for all of us, by making it possible to approach salient problems in a personal, although not private, way . . . fiction accomplishes the feat which organization theory often misses: it combines the subjective with the objective, the fate of individuals with that of institutions, the micro events with the macro systems[1] .

Dwight Waldo has contributed a great deal of his wisdom to the study of administration. He also appreciates fiction. He tells us that the social scientist and the writer of stories function in two different worlds. Each has something to give that the other cannot. In the modern world, we are all aware of what the scientist contributes to progress. Yet a more complete understanding of the complex ways in which the human condition and administrative structures mix, claims Waldo, requires the insight and the imagination that is brought to us by the teller of stories. Waldo suggests that the administrative scientist and the teller of stories each has a distinct contribution to make. The former can tell us most about the situation and problems of the system. The latter, since he or she looks at life from the bias of the individual and examines life at a level of analysis of the individual, can tell us more about the situation and the problem of the individual.[2]

Waldo also tells us that there is a fine line between our accumulation of experience and our reflection on fiction. He writes that "An imaginative construction may flow from much personal experience, and a good one almost of necessity does; a reconstruction from memory will inevitably have have a fictional component."[3]

The study of fictional cases is a useful complement to experience. Waldo also points out that the study of fiction can reveal a much more elegant and complete portrayal of the organizational landscape. He says that " Here we have an opportunity to observe, under widely differing conditions and in varying perspectives, a "whole" situation, one in which politics (or policy) and administration are joined by an act of artistic synthesis rather than separated by an act of scientific analysis."[4] Waldo goes on to tell us that science experiments by controlling variables, an all other things being equal methodology. If the scientist wants to determine the impact of a medicine on a disease he has to arrange his experiment by controlling for factors that may be affecting outcomes other than the medicine, factors such as the age of subjects, the health history of subjects, and the genetic make up of subjects. In a fictional story which explains the meaning of our non-fictional lives, however, all other things are not equal. Fiction can thereby capture the full complexity of circumstance in a way that is not readily available to the scientific method, but is produced by the method of art.

Whereas Waldo emphasizes the separate perspectives of science and art, Charles Goodsell and Nancy Murray [5] suggest that useful conceptual bridges can be constructed to span the perceived gulfs that separate the rational and scientific study of administration and the arts. The description and analysis of stories examined in subsequent chapters will build some of these bridges.

First of all is the bridge that connects theory and the arts. Aesthetic inquiry considers the individual's place in an overarching view of beauty (and by implication ugliness). The stories discussed here all focus on the relationship of the individual to his circumstance and environment. This can lead to a deeper understanding, a capacity to make sense of the organizational system.

A second bridge pertains to values. Fictional stories teach us insights not normally attainable in the classroom or on the job. Stories translate into a concrete form based on those concepts that are norm-laden such as power, ambition, survival and vision. Careful examination and analysis encourages us to examine our own values and to evaluate our own situations in ways that we would not otherwise contemplate.

Goodsell and Murray's teaching bridge is also relevant to the process of sensemaking and self discovery. They tell us that "Enthusiasts of administrative fiction have argued for some years that one of the few ways we have to transmit the subtleties of administrative processes to novice students [and I would add to seasoned practitioners] in an otherwise sterile classroom is through novels or film." [6]

Examination of the stories told in the following chapters results in vicarious experience and can help build on intuitive survival skills. Moreover, consideration of film stories as cases can illuminate important and powerful abstractions, can make them accessible and relevant to the lives of the viewer. These vicarious experiences can help us to use our imagination to make progress toward the discovery of our authentic selves and to pursue our natural work.

Chapter Ten

Getting Lost and Finding Yourself

To study the abnormal is the best way of understanding the normal,

William James

The film *Lost in America*[1] tells us the story of David and Linda. This twenty something couple graduated from college eight years ago. As so many college students do they thought about living a life free of the constraints of the corporation world; they thought about cutting the chains that bound them to what they considered to be crass materialism. The lure of upward economic and social status, however, attracted them more to the middle class mainstream than to life as free spirits. The story of the journey of David and Linda involves getting lost and finding themselves on a long their journey to self discovery.

At the start of the story David and Linda are upwardly mobile urban dwellers living in Los Angeles. David is the artistic director of an advertising firm, one of the biggest. Linda works in the Human Resource Department of a department store.

David is a candidate for promotion to Executive Vice President. He has been climbing the corporate ladder for eight years and considers this promotion to be the jewel in his professional crown. He is so sure of this promotion that he is negotiating for the purchase of a new Mercedes and has gone into escrow to purchase a luxury home. When he complains to Linda that "Our new house will not have a tennis court!" his wife replies, "But you don't even play tennis." He responds, "If you have a tennis court your learn.

Indeed David has much to learn, not so much about tennis as about himself and about the possible difference between what he is and what the corporation wants him to be.

Linda recognizes that David is treading an unknown and possibly problematic path. She tells a colleague that for years David has climbed the ladder of seniority and at each step he has proclaimed that "If I just get this, everything will be all right." His track record is one of achieving career goals and setting new and higher goals, but the more he drinks of success, the thirstier he gets. Linda is not at all sure that all will be right and that they will live happily ever after.

David meets with his boss. He is joyfully expecting the news that he is being promoted to Executive Vice President. David, however, is informed that he will be assigned to the newly acquired Ford account and transferred from the home office in Los Angeles to New York. Much to David's horror, his colleague is being promoted to Executive Vice President. The corporation, David is told, needs his creative talent in New York.

David's disappointment is devastating. Failure to get this promotion is a rude awakening, one of those surprises that upsets the applecart of his expectations. He can make no sense at all of his transfer to the New York Office. He turns from a cooperative *Dr. Jekel* into a raving *Mr. Hyde*. He throws a temper tantrum, quits his job and is simultaneously fired

As we consider the ideas concerning sensemaking discussed in chapter eight, we should keep in mind that this surprise will form for David a frame of reference within which he can place subsequent events. This should help him to make sense of the twists and turns of the road that leads him to get *Lost in America*. This should help him to find his authentic self and perhaps lead him to a job where he can labor at his natural work.

Faced with the present disappointment, David decides to reject the conventional urban middle class life style. He is now free of the shackles of corporate America. He can now become a free spirit.

He convinces Linda to quit her job. David and Linda sell all their assets, buy a large motor home and set off to recover their freedom by traveling across the country. "I want to touch an Indian," proclaims David.

As they set off on a journey of exploration the couple stops at Las Vegas to affirm their love by remarrying at an all night wedding chapel. They check into a hotel.

While David sleeps Linda slips out of their room and heads for the casino. During a farewell to what she now considers to be the false values of modern civilization, Linda, who has not yet had a chance to savor the release of a temper tantrum the way that David has, gambles away almost all the cash (the nest egg) that David and she have acquired to support their anticipated free spirited life style.

Linda has lived a life of pent-up aspirations. When her secretary discussed her impending move into a large and luxurious home Linda remarked, "You know, I am going to hate this house." She does not know why. Her desire to be fulfilled has been frustrated by the fact that she has no idea what will make her happy. The significant stash of cash that she acquired as the result of liquidating the couple's assets does not make her feel any better than she did in the first place. She justifies her seemingly irrational gambling behavior by explaining to a shocked David that poverty frees one from responsibility.

Now David and Linda have just enough cash and gas to get them to a trailer park in rural Arizona. Their only option is to find jobs so that they can survive. The best David can do is sign on as a crossing guard at a school where wise guy students torment him. When a city fellow drives by in a Mercedes and asks directions to Los Angeles, David asks him if he likes the car. The reply is, "What's not to like?" We see the look on David's face. What is not to like indeed! David can see that there is much to like.

The best job that Linda can find is as an assistant manager in a fast food restaurant. Her boss is an enthusiastic adolescent who condescends to let David and Linda address him by his first name, Skippy.

When Linda tells Skippy that the french fries he is serving are not quite defrosted, Skippy sees Linda as a managerial genius. "That's quite a wife you've got there," Skippy informs David.

The humiliation of Skippy's assumption of the role of the couple's guru is the last straw. David and Linda simultaneously come to the conclusion that life in rural Arizona is not the life for them. They decide to go to New York to get back into the mainstream of urban professionalism.

When David and Linda reach New York, David goes to work on the Ford account, albeit at a reduction in salary, but with medical benefits. Linda starts work for a department store and has a child.

By the end of the story David and Linda have come to the realization that what they want is what they had all along, a cosmopolitan lifestyle. Their problem was that they did not understand themselves. They had what they wanted, but they could not appreciate what they had. Getting *Lost in America* enabled them to understand their need for the comfort, prestige, and the security of economic accomplishment, a need that could only be provided by an urban corporate environment.

As we think about this story we should consider that David and Linda experience two wake up calls. The first is David's failure to be promoted. The second is Skippy, the young fast food restaurant manager, taking on the role of guru-mentor. We see David and Linda in New York at the end of the story. Of course, that is not the end of their lives. They have altered the course on their life journey. The journey, however, is far from over. We are left with the questions:

- What next?" and "What then?"
- Has David found his natural work ?
- Do we have to get lost before we can find our authentic selves and the work that is an end in itself rathe than a means to an end?
- Is the frame of reference that David forms as a result of his disappointment in Los Angeles a catalyst to his capacity to make sense of his experience?
- Is Linda now closer to understanding what it will take to make her happy?

Chapter Eleven

Listen to the Horse

The souls of horses mirror the souls of men more closely than men suppose

Cormac McCarthy

As we act out the events that make up the story of our lives, we play the roles that are driven by our needs. Some of these needs are common to all people. Some of these are unique to our particular selves. For the action of our lives to *work*, i.e. to be satisfying to ourselves, we must have a profound understanding of what it is we *are* in the first place. Unlike the actors in films we have neither writer nor director to guide us in this important task. The screen writer and the director tell the actors that portray David and Linda in the film *Lost in America* what they are, how to act. For us to find out what we are, however, can be a much more tortuous process. The story told by the film *Electric Horseman* [1] gives us another look at how a wake up call, a crisis, can lead to sensemaking that results in self discovery.

Sonny Steele is the *Electric Horseman.* His past glory as a champion rodeo cowboy has faded. He has become an aging spokesman for a corporation. He hawks breakfast cereal at shopping center promotional events and high school half-time football game shows. He has commercialized himself, become a *product.* Sonny attempts to escape from the pain of the physical injuries sustained in rodeo days and the emotional pain of corporate bondage by turning to a life a booze and casual sex. Sonny has, in the words of his ex-wife, "...lost the best part of himself."

Rising Star is a magnificent stallion whose past glory on the racetrack has also faded. Sonny and the horse come together as fellow corporate employees. The washed-out cowboy is to ride the has-been stallion in a glitzy Las Vegas review staged by the corporation to promote its product. Sonny sees that the horse has been pumped full of steroids and tranquilizers. He sees the wreck of what was the soul of the horse. He sees himself.

In a masterful display of horsemanship and equine endurance Sonny and Rising Star unite to defect from their corporate masters with: an amazing ride through a hotel casino, a wild chase by police cruisers through the streets of Las Vegas, and a dash across rugged and desolate terrain. By the time Sonny and Rising Star reach a secret place populated by herds of wild horses, both the man and the stallion are ready to begin new lives.

Rising Star is turned loose and is out from under the *protection* and control of man. Sonny no longer has the security of a steady job, but both horse and man are much closer to, more in harmony with, whatever is the essence of their being, the best part of themselves.

When I asked my students to think about the situation of Sonny and to answer the question, "What is his problem?" one insightful student answered, "The corporation has *uncowboyed* him." After some discussion the class interpreted that statement to mean that the essence of Sonny's values could be captured by the role *cowboy* and that his employer required him to ignore this role and play one that was antithetical to it.

The role of *cowboy* captures the image of the generic mythical figure that we see displayed on the screen in classic western movies. It also reveals the inner-self of Sonny, the characteristics that define what he *is*: a rugged individual, a man who loves the freedom of the outdoors, who dislikes actual as well as metaphoric fences, a man who is willing to take risks, a man who is fiercely loyal to friends.

The pain of failure to understand a person's self and the epiphany of self discovery are common themes in stories about the relationship between organizations and the people who inhabit them. Often the bearer of the mandates to "know thyself and "to thine own self be true" comes in the form of an interaction with and an empathy for another species. In the case of Sonny Steele it is a horse. This is appropriate because (so called) lower species behave as though they have a full understanding of what it is they are and what behavior is appropriate to their survival and happiness. The animal plays out his natural repertoire of attitude and behavior because nature "hard wires" him to play a very specific role, that of a *horse*. When the horse is domesticated and his human master does not take his natural role into account the horse can act in neurotic and self destructive ways.

Man, on the other hand, has the faculty of self-consciousness and free will, the power constantly to "reprogram" himself. Indeed the search for his authentic "program", his nature, is a central element of man's experience of life. More often than not, he finds himself pushing against whatever is his own nature, his own soul. Life for many men and women is a process of trial and error, an attempt to find the self that is the synthesis of human nature and man made experience, the *real* self. Another film illustrates this point quite clearly.

The film *In Pursuit of Honor*[2] tells the tale of two rebellious cavalry soldiers during the Great Depression. Down and out World War I Army veterans are protesting the government's decision to withhold promised bonuses. Sergeant Libby becomes a maverick when he refuses to use his horse to put down the protest by terrorizing his fellow soldiers. The organization has assigned him the role of *policeman.* The role he wants to play, a role that is more authentic for him, is that of *comrade.*

Lieutenant Buxton has been sent to a dead-end remote post because he struck a fellow officer who abused a horse. Libby has also been exiled to the post. In the same way that the horse was Sonny Steele's connection to his calling of *cowboy* so is the horse a connection to the soldiers' identity as *cavalry men.* Indeed the army horses run to muster from their pasture at the sound of a bugle; the base commander refers to himself as "...an old war horse." It is their mutual love of horses that creates a bond of friendship between Libby and Buxton and a bond between these two and the Army.

The identity of both men, the role of both men as *horse soldiers,* is undermined when the usefulness and practicality of the cavalry horse is overcome by technical progress and circumstance. Budget constraints of a peacetime army, belt tightening of *The Great Depression*, and the advent of mechanized means of transport and fighting all lead to downsizing. This means destroying large numbers of horses.

We witness the machine gunning of one hundred horses. The sight revolts the viewer. It also disgusts our two heroes. The Lieutenant proclaims "This smacks of insanity." Buxton and Libby stampede the remaining 400 horses and flee to the desert, just as Sonny Steele fled with Rising Star. The police cars in pursuit of Steele were no match for the horse. The machines of the army cannot thwart the dash of the herd for life. Neither can these machines block the soldiers escape from the insanity of the army. In the end, the rebellious soldiers and the horses make it to Canada where the 400 hundred rescued army mounts will be given to an Indian tribe.

In each of these movies, what the human and the horse *does* is controlled by a modern institution: the corporation, the army. The institution has become the master of the values of the individual. The men have unwittingly given up part of themselves in order to join civilization. It is the same with the horse. The cost of joining civilization is the destruction of whatever it is they *are*: *cavalry man*, *cowboy*, *horse*. Each of these identities is made up of values that suit and are in harmony with the inner man or the natural horse. Each of these identities personifies the soul, the *self* of the human or the creature.

In these stories, the horse helps to recreate the integrity of the man, to bring him closer to what he is. It is the plight of the horse that informs the man that his soul is in trouble. It is the natural instinct of the horse for flight that suggests to the man the solution to his problem.

Chapter Twelve

Living a Whole Life

His own heart laughed; and that was quite enough for him,

Charles Dickens, <u>A Christmas Carol</u>

In the previous chapter we witnessed the journey to self-discovery as the result of a dramatic and severe crisis, one that could hardly go unrecognized or unmanaged. Yet most of us would not consciously place ourselves in the boots of Sonny Steele, or of the two calvary men, or for that matter in the position of David as a crossing guard, or Linda as an assistant to Skippy. We do not *search* for trauma as a mechanism of sensemaking and self discovery.

Most of us spend a great deal of thought and energy attempting to place ourselves in situations where crises never invade our working lives. A strategy of crisis avoidance, and indeed risk avoidance, seems to be rational. It is not at all apparent that going through a spate of unhappiness can be a prescription for achieving happiness. Rather than trying to achieve a state of happiness we try to avoid unhappiness, we try to be content. The important distinction between contentment and happiness may go unnoticed. Our *potential* for happiness may therefore go unrecognized. We become complacent. The option of living our organizational lives in *quiet* desperation may be one we choose heedlessly. Quiet desperation, however can be a fertile ground for hidden misery.

In literature, the quintessential unhappy man who suffers from and then transcends misery that is hidden from his own perception is Charles Dickens' *Scrooge,* the main character in his novel *A Christmas Carol.*[1] The fantasy of Scrooge's unintended careful examination of his own life, of his own behavior, is a story that is retold in a different but equally fantastic form in the film *Groundhog Day.*[2]

This story takes place on February 2, Groundhog Day, indeed during a long series of Groundhog days. This is the day when, in Punxsutawney Pennsylvania, the groundhog Phil leaves his den. If he sees his shadow, there will be six more weeks of winter.

Phil Conners is a TV weather man at a small station in Pittsburgh. He does not respect the low status of the organization that employs him. He brags that "There is a major network interested in me."

The weather man and his crew are leaving on assignment to cover the story of the emergence of the groundhog. The mundane nature of this assignment is not up to the level of prestige that he expects. Phil happily informs his coworkers, producer Rita and camera man Larry, that this is the last time he is going to have to do the Groundhog Festival.

The crew of three travels to Punxsutawney. Phil stays at an upscale Bed and Breakfast while producer and camera man stay at a lesser place. He justifies this by saying that "You have to keep the talent happy." This is our first hint concerning Phil's problem. He perceives that to be happy, he has to be aloof and isolated from others.

Phil is not consciously distressed. In this respect, his situation is significantly different from that of Sonny Steele. Whatever it was that made Sonny Steele unhappy was not far from the surface. That's why Sonny had to keep beating himself up with numbing alcohol and distracting sex. Sonny was far from consciously content. On the other hand, if there is a separation between what Phil is and what he does, the separation is so wide, the authentic nature of Phil buried so deeply below the surface, below his conscious sense of himself, that it remains unrecognized and unmanaged.

Like Scrooge, Phil is angry with everyone; he walks around with a very large chip on his shoulder. He utters the proverbial "bah humbug" in many different ways.

It is 6AM on February 2. Phil's alarm clock radio turns on. The song is Sonny and Cher with *I Got You Babe*. Phil goes downstairs to breakfast. He humiliates the innkeeper by demanding Cappuccino when she does not even know what that is. He has to settle for just a plain cup of coffee.

On the way to cover the festival he encounters a high school chum, Ned. Ned is an insurance salesman. He gives Ned the brush off. Ned is just another inferior person. Phil steps in a cold puddle of water. He is not paying attention to anything. His mind is elsewhere. He would rather be elsewhere. He is just as mad at the place as he is at the people. At the site of the Groundhog Day festivities Phil meets up with Rita and Larry. Phil proclaims his disdain for the people of the town. "They're hicks, Rita" he proclaims.

At 7:29 the groundhog comes out and sees his shadow. There will be six more weeks of winter. Phil as weather man has predicted a milder weather. This is contrary to the groundhog's prediction. Once again it is the animal, the child of nature, who honestly responds to the truth of nature. This contrasts with man who fools himself and becomes a victim of self-delusion. Phil would rather listen to himself than be the slightest bit inspired by the animal or by the myth of the animal's weather forecasting prowess.

Contrary to the weather man's prediction, there is a blizzard. The groundhog is correct. The storm prevents the TV crew from returning to Pittsburgh. They are stuck in Punxsutawney. Phil is not in control of his circumstances, but he wants to be. He says, "I make the weather." There is something deep inside Phil that is simmering with frustration. His desire to control nature, perhaps even his own human nature, is thwarted. His reaction to this frustration is to deny it, to push it as far below the surface of his consciousness as he can.

It is 6AM, and it should be the next day. Phil's alarm radio goes off. Once again we hear the refrain of *I Got You Babe*. The exact same scenario as the previous day is replayed: the humiliation of the innkeeper, the brush off of his high school chum. It is still the same day!

Phil is aware that he is repeating the same day, but none of the other characters are cognizant of this. Just as Scrooge had to relive a portion of his previous Christmases, so Phil now relives the same Groundhog Day... over and over and over again.

Phil attempts to cope with the anxiety and unpleasantness of the repeated day by recalling a great day he had on vacation in the Virgin Islands. That was like the Garden of Eden. He relaxed. He made love. "Why couldn't I get *that* day over?" he asks.

Phil is locked in his job and his lifestyle, locked in a state of quiet desperation, in a state of hidden misery. We have seen another indication of Phil's hidden misery, his yearning for the days that he had time off. This brings to mind the common phenomenon of spending working hours yearning for the week-end or the vacation.

Phil's occupation as a TV weather man is not a source of any real satisfaction. His work is not at all an end in and of itself. It is only a means to the end of occasional leisure and increased status. Leisure, at least for Phil, is a temporary fix that wears off the moment he is back on the job. Like David in *Lost In America*, the goal of increased status once achieved will prove to be an meaningless shadow, devoid of substance.

It is not so much that Phil's purpose has come into direct conflict with his TV station organization. Unlike Colonel Davenport, (in the film *Twelve O'clock High*) who desires to preserve the lives of his men in spite of General Prichard's unswerving dedication to using daylight precision bombing to help win the war, unlike Sonny Steele, who desperately seeks to preserve the soul of his cowboy self, unlike David, who recognizes that his cosmopolitan life style may satisfy his inner needs, Phil has no purpose at all, no value that he seeks to satisfy. When he punches at life it is like punching a bag of feathers. No pressure sent in return can signal him to make adjustments that might be beneficial to his state of mind. He is not able to take care of his own soul.

Phil does not perceive that he has a problem. There is no wake up call to wake him up, no frame of reference that can enable him to make sense of his unhappiness. He is living inside the trap of a reality that he has constructed for himself. What is the reality that Phil perceives? What is the cause of his hidden misery? How does this relate to his situation as a member of an organization?

Phil's behavior is antisocial. He perceives that there is nothing rewarding in accepting a role as a team player. His membership in the organization is valid in a formal sense, but does not affect his attitude or the way he behaves. He experiences the loneliness of the loner because he is interested only in individual outcomes, only what happens to him. He fails to see that by cooperating with others he would be more effective at his job and be more satisfied by his work. He fails to see that by interacting in a positive way with others he can be happier. He fails to see that the human connection with others can be an activity that is an end in and of itself.

The words of Charles Dickens as he describes Scrooge might just as well have been said of Phil:

> Oh! But he was a tight-fisted hand at the grindstone, Scrooge! a squeezing, wrenching, grasping, clutching, covetous old sinner! Hard and sharp as flint, from which no steel had ever struck out generous fire; secret, and self-contained, and solitary as an oyster.

As Phil lives the same Groundhog Day over and over again he reveals to us that he wants very much to repudiate the rules made by others, the mandates of others, the specification of others for living a life that is good. Previously, he had to live by the rules of others or suffer the consequences. Now the fantasy of the story places him in a situation where there is no tomorrow and it is only when tomorrow arrives that the rule-breaker suffers the consequences of his behavior. Accordingly, Phil has an opportunity to play out his most urgent fantasy, his most egotistical desire : the rejection, without risk to himself, of the guidelines that define civilization, that specify the correct response, the correct relationship, of one human being in an organized system to another and the relationship of the individual to the social or organizational system as a whole.

Phil proclaims, "It is the same thing all your life...Be nice to your sister....Sometime you have to take big chances". He announces, "I am not going to live by their rules anymore."

He meets Ned and punches him. This is assault, but by the next morning the assault did not happen. He eats unhealthy food. Why not? There are no consequences. He lets his cholesterol rise. He smokes. He proclaims,"I don't even have to floss." He drives wildly, defying the police and waking up the next morning, i.e. the same morning, without having to face the consequences of his defiance of the law. "I don't worry about anything anymore" he says. This statement reveals what Phil's worry has been all along, the source of his self-imposed isolation: his fear of loosing control of his own life as the result of having to live in a manner that is prescribed by others.

The story now gives Phil a way out of the trap of his own personal reality, a reality of the world as a demanding place where only an unsympathetic isolated person can survive and maintain his sanity. The unseen *Fairy Godmother*, or whatever supernatural being the viewer chooses to imagine, gives Phil the gift of freedom. This gift relieves him of the necessity to protect himself from the perceived harshness of mankind, gives him the capacity to experiment with his own life, starts him on the road from hidden misery to happiness. Clearly, if we perceive that we have no freedom, no control over our own lives, we have no chance to discover our authentic selves.

The capacity of each person to take chances, to experiment with his life and the desirability of doing so, weaves its way through the stories that help us to understand the necessity of discovering our authentic selves. General Savage took a big chance when he held up the pilot's requests for transfer. Sonny took a big chance when he rode off with Rising Star. The calvary men took a big chance when they fled with the doomed horses. David and Linda took a big chance when they went off to "touch an Indian." These chances are all part of a pattern of experimentation a pattern of following a road that is not defined by a course through life which is plotted by others.

Like many of our fictional characters, Phil needs to break away from the reality, the rules, of others, the map that is drawn by others before he can find himself. In this way he can learn to accept responsibility for his own happiness, gain control of his own life, escape from having to defend himself from what he perceives is the nasty and brutish existence caused by "...their rules."

One February 2 turns into the next, and the next and the next....Phil's experiment places him on a power trip. He even dresses up as the hero in one of those Italian western movies, the *Spaghetti Western*, whose characters are even more macho and powerful than the ordinary western hero portrayed in the American Westerns.

Now that Phil has established that he does not have to obey the rules of others, to fear the rules of others, he experiments by using the fantasy of his circumstances to control others.

Nancy Taylor is a very pretty woman who Phil would like to know. The old antisocial Phil would have been inept at making contact. The new Phil has a tool that the old Phil did not have: the capacity to obtain information about people and to use this to manipulate them. By coming into contact with Nancy each repeated day and having a short conversation with her he learns about her. He uses this information to cajole Nancy into believing that she knows him as a former but forgotten school mate. "I even asked you to the prom," he says.

When he makes love to Nancy, he cries out to Rita, his producer. The intensity of sex has started to break the barrier between his surface self and his inner emotions. It is clear that his hidden emotions focus on a desire for Rita.

As he works his way through the phases of defiance and power, Phil's deep feelings for Rita emerge. The door which enables him to escape from his hidden misery is opening. He reaches out to Rita. He asks her, "If you only had one day to live, what would you do with it?"

Rita tells Phil what she wants: a man who is intelligent and supportive, kind, sensitive, gentle. She tells him that she likes animals, that she wants to change dirty diapers. Phil interacts with Rita the same way that he did with Nancy, by gathering information that he can use. He finds out what Rita's favorite drink is during a date on one day so he can order the same drink for himself during the same date replayed. He imitates Rita's favorite man. Rita wants world peace. He toasts world peace. She is interested in 19th century French poetry. He recites some for her. Phil, of course, is faking it. He is interested neither in world peace nor in French poetry.

Usually we think of faking as a negative behavior, dishonest. In the context of Phil's experiment, it is positive. On the first day of many of my classes, I tell college students that a *requirement* of the course is that they be interested in the course material. I advise them that if they are not interested, they should fake interest. When they finish laughing or staring at me in amazement, I explain that sometimes faking it means giving something a chance in a way that you have not done before. Once you do this, I go on, maybe you will discover that you enjoy and are interested in the material after all.

Phil's imitation of Rita's favorite man has the impact on Phil I have suggested to my students. As he experiments, he starts genuinely to appreciate something new. For Phil, the something new is spontaneity. He is beginning a transformation. He will become someone like the Scrooge Dickens describes once the ghosts of the past have shown him the causes of his own hidden misery.

> "I don't know what day of the month it is!" said Scrooge. "I don't know how long I've been among the Spirits. I don't know anything. I'm quite a baby. Never mind. I don't care. I'd rather be a baby.

Phil joins Rita in a snowball fight with some local children. He dances with Rita and discovers the joy of the contact and the rhythm. Phil has played the role of a mean and nasty person as a way of dealing with the conflict between his inner-self and his surface-self. He acts negatively, but he also has the impulse to reach out and share his life with well-adjusted people like Rita.

We have already observed the discomfort of Phil's mind set in others, e.g. Sonny Steele's authentic self as a cowboy is in conflict with his role of a salesman. One way of dealing with this sort of conflict, of making all aspects of your feelings and behavior match up, as compared to being dissonant, is to act out one of the roles and reject the other. Sonny did this in his own way. He accepts the cowboy self and rejects the salesman. Phil's way has been to act out the role of the nasty person and bury the nice guy. He can't throw away the nice guy like Sonny threw away the salesman until the fantasy of the story empowers him to do so.

Phil learns that he has choices. He can experiment with different roles. He can create different situations in the same way David and Linda played around with their lives. He tries something he was afraid to try before. At the end of a perfect day with Rita, Phil kisses her and tells her that he loves her. Somehow Rita realizes that she has been taken advantage of. "I can't believe I fell for this," she says. She leaves him.

Since the next day is the same day. He has a chance to have another perfect day with her. He tries the same day over and over again and at the end of each day she slaps his face. The song *But You Don't Know Me* played on the sound track at this point gives us a hint concerning Rita's motivation for the continuing rejection of Phil.

Phil's first attempt at getting close to Rita has failed. He experiments with self-destructive behavior. He kidnaps the groundhog and drives off a cliff. No problem— the next day offers him another chance. He commits suicide by throwing a toaster in his bathtub. He jumps from a tower. He lives to experiment another day.

Phil is invulnerable. He says that he is "a god" and makes the comment that "... maybe the real God knows everything. Maybe he's just been around so long he knows everything." This is the insight that finally empowers Phil to escape from his hidden misery. Phil's experimentation leads to a life affirming conclusion. He has discovered that knowledge, even wisdom, is the result of experience. Up to now his experience has been limited by his own fear and lack of self-esteem. The plot of the fantasy has given him the chance to become a god....i.e. to become his authentic self. Rita is the catalyst for the emergence of Phil's godliness.

Phil complains to Rita that having to live the same day over and over is a curse. She tells him that maybe it is a blessing. The date that they have lived over and over again ends with her coming to his room in the Bed and Breakfast hotel. She stays with him. At 6 am, however, it is the same day again and she is gone.

On the way to cover the continuing series of Groundhog Day ceremonies Phil gives money to a homeless beggar. He is friendly to all he meets. He pays $1000 for a piano lesson. He carves an ice sculpture. There is an artist in Phil who is starting to emerge. He finds a role within himself that he had not previously imagined.

Because he has been living the same day over and over, each piano lesson is his first. Because Phil carries the experience of each lesson into the next, i.e. the same, day he gets better and better. He uses the experience of the lesson to evoke the artist in him.

He meets Ned and gives him a big hug. Here is the role of "friend" emerging. An old homeless man dies. Phil looks at the chart in the hospital to which the body of the old man has been transported in hopes of saving him the next day. The old man dies, however, dies again despite Phil's attempt to save his life. Phil realizes that even with his seemingly magical powers he cannot control everything. There may be godliness in him, but he is not God.

Phil can reap the benefits of his godliness, improve his self-esteem. There is a hero deep inside Phil. He needs to get others to recognize and to validate the hero. Only then can he recognize the hero in himself. He saves a boy who falls from a tree. He changes a flat tire for stranded women. He saves the Mayor from choking to death by administering first aid. He uses his newly acquired musical skills to dazzle the celebrants at a Groundhog Day party.

At the party the women of the town bid in an auction for the company of bachelors. The proceeds will go to charity. Rita, having observed Phil's good deeds, realizes she is in love with him. She bids $339.88, all she has, and wins his company.

Phil carves an ice statue in Rita's image. Phil says that no matter what happens tomorrow, he is happy.

It is 6AM, Phil wakes up. This time, however, Rita is still in bed next to him. He proclaims, "Something is different." Indeed it is. This is the next day. The ground is covered with snow. It is tomorrow.

Phil says "Let's live here." The story ends to the refrain of the song *It's Almost Like Being in Love*.

At first glance the film *Groundhog Day* is a lighthearted comedy. As we have seen, however, much in the way of useful understanding can be gleaned from taking a closer look at Phil, who is forced by a fantastic set of circumstances more closely to examine himself and his relationship with the social and organizational systems with which he is in contact.

As a teacher, I can certainly relate to living the same semester, if not the same day, over and over. Burnout can be a professional hazard of teaching, or of any occupation, just as Phil was burned out by his yearly visits to the Punxsutawney. Each academic year I am a year older. Yet the students' faces seem to remain the same. I set up shop in the same classrooms, deal with the same problems, repeat the same processes.

This repetition, as it was for Phil, can for me be a source of enlightenment and pleasure, but only as I pay careful attention. Each semester is the same. Each semester is different. If I can recognize the differences in my behavior and the way in which I am either more effective or less effective; if I can recognize the way that changes in my behavior affect my own satisfaction, I can close the gap between the purpose of myself, that of my students and the purpose of my organization. By paying attention to

Socrates' admonition to live an examined life I can come one step closer to my inner self and to the sort of joy that Phil finally discovers.

Phil found out that life can be a grand experiment, where knowledge and wisdom can be harvested as the result of experience, even repeated experience. Perhaps Phil hit the nail right on the head when he speculated that God knows everything because he has been around so long.

Chapter Thirteen

Playing a Role

It matters not how strait the gate
How charged with punishments the scroll,
I am the master of my fate:
I am the captain of my soul

W.E . Henley

Paying attention to repeated experience is one way that we can live an examined life and benefit from that examination. Another strategy for discovering one's authentic self is to pay attention to the problem of role conflict and learn from the way that we respond this aspect of the human condition.

A significant obstacle that confounds the work in progress of discovering our authentic selves is that our motivation and behavior are often driven by sets of values that make up more than one role. When it is difficult or impossible to integrate multiple roles we are stressed by the pulls and hauls of role conflict. When this happens we need to choose one role or another to relieve tension. The role that we choose as we try to make sense out of complexity and conflict tells us something about the nature of our authentic self.

Sonny Steele (in the film story *Electric Horseman*) found that his cowboy set of values were in conflict with his persona as a corporate symbol, a role that gave him the advantage of steady pay. David (in *Lost In*

America) similarly experienced the inner conflict between his role as a corporate executive and his desire to conform to the ideals that motivated him upon graduation from college. Role conflict involves the pulls and hauls that can compete for the possession of person's soul.

Role conflict is resolved when we unambiguously chooses one preferred role. That choice tells us something about the nature of our authentic self, the authentic role that we need to play if we are to pursue goals that are ends in and of themselves, goals the achievement of which result in happiness.

David rejected the role of freewheeling gypsy and accepted the role of *corporate midlevel executive* because he needed to resolve his inner conflict. The organization provided him a way out of his dilemma. Sonny Steele chooses the *cowboy* role as comprising the values that represent his authentic self. General Savage, in *Twelve O'clock High* does the same thing when he attempts to assume the singular role of *General* by rejecting the *Father* role which would motivate him to consider the safety of aircrews as a highest priority. Davenport, on the other hand, lets down the organization when he rejects the role of *Colonel* to be comfortable with his persona as fatherly protector of comrades.

The exclusive focus on one role, one consistent set of values, can become a form of coping with the emotional stress of role conflict, as well as a way of making sense out of a situation that is uncomfortably complex. Of course, Savage's choice of rejecting the role of *Father* gets him in emotional trouble. This should alert him to the fact that his organizational role as a leader may satisfy some of his needs but that ultimately he is going to have to deal with the fact that what the organization wants of him conflicts with what his needs as a human being. The story told by the film *A Few Good Men*[1] is another example of how the resolution of role conflict leads to self understanding.

As a result of the 1898 American victory in the Spanish-American war, the United States was given a 99 year renewable lease to build a base at Guantanamo Bay, Cuba. When Fidel Castro became the Cuban leader and declared himself a Marxist, the enclave of the U.S. military base became a hot spot of the Cold War. In this story the perimeter of the base is lined with a fence manned by stalwart Marines, armed sentries who stand between the free world and the Communist hordes. Of course, the Cubans have an equal number of their own riflemen in position to protect their own world from the Americans.

A young Marine, Private Willie Santiago, witnesses one of his comrades taking gratuitous pot shots at his opposite number (mirror) on the Cuban side of the fence. He assumes the role of the whistle blower and reports this violation of the formal rules of engagement: *Do not fire unless fired upon.* Such rules are not formulated by the Marine's organization on the base... Rifle Security Company, Marine Barracks Windward, Guantanamo Bay Cuba. They are imposed by higher command. The civilian political arm of the government must control the management of violence. The job of the Marines is to be able to shoot well. The job of the civilian politicians representing American society is to tell Marines when to shoot and who to shoot.

When Private Santiago's complaints are ignored by his Commanding Officer, Colonel Nathan Jessup, Santiago writes to his Congressman. By doing so he ignores the chain-of-command. Private Santiago has violated the informal rules, the code designed to encourage group cohesiveness: *Marines do not rat on each other; Marines do not go outside of the chain-of-command.*

Because Santiago has behaved so badly, i.e. gone outside the chain-of -command, Colonel Jessup must now sanction the young Marine. Jessup is advised by his second-in-command, Lieutenant Colonel Markensen, to ship Santiago back to the mainland. Santiago is in danger, Markensen believes, of bodily harm inflicted by his comrades because he has violated the code. Jessup rejects this advice. If a Marine shows weakness in any form, his seniors must lead him down the proper path, must make him strong. Colonel Jessup proclaims that "We have a responsibility to this country to see that the men and women charged with its security are trained professionals." "Transfer," he says," is not, in a manner of speaking, the American way!"

Santiago must be taught a lesson and the tool to do this is Code Red, hazing in the form of physical punishment administered by peers. Colonel Jessup orders Lieutenant Kendrick, Santiago's platoon commander, to administer a Code Red. Kendrick surreptitiously passes this order along to Corporal Dawson and Private Downey. Dawson and Downey push a rag into Santiago's mouth to keep him quiet during the administration of a beating. Santiago, who is not in good shape to start with, suffers an attack of lactic acidosis and dies, drowning in his own blood.

A Navy doctor erroneously proclaims that Santiago's death must have been the result of poison on the rag stuffed into his mouth by Dawson and Downey. This is the first step in a coverup designed to protect Colonel Jessup and Lieutenant Kendrick, to protect the Marine Corps. The Colonel and the Lieutenant falsely deny that the Code Red was ordered by them.

The two young marines who were, in fact, following the orders of their seniors, are indicted for murder. The defense lawyer in the court martial of Dawson and Downey is a young Navy Judge Advocate General Officer, a recent graduate of Harvard Law School, Lieutenant Junior Grade Caffey. Caffey is an expert at plea bargaining. In this case, however, he rejects this defense strategy more out of his own hubris than any solid legal logic.

The two young Marines plead innocent by virtue of having been given an order originating with Colonel Jessup. If they are found guilty they will spend the rest of their lives in a military prison.

The only witness who can testify that Santiago's death was caused by Colonel Jessup is Lieutenant Colonel Markensen. Jessup's second-in-command is aware of the cover up. Markensen, however, feels profoundly guilty because he did not protect Santiago by preventing the Code Red action. He feels that his own weakness is the cause of Santiago's death. He commits suicide and Caffey is left without a witness to prove his case.

Naval Officer/ Lawyer Caffey's only recourse is to call Colonel Jessup to the stand. Jessup has informed Caffey "We are in the business of saving lives." Jessup has told Caffey that he "...eats breakfast 400 yards from Cubans who are trained to kill me." Caffey perceives that the Colonel's self-image as a valiant and heroic warrior is the chink in his armor. He believes that Jessup is proud of having ordered the Code Red. He feels that Jessup conceives of the Code Red as the right thing to do. Caffey perceives that Jessup believes himself to be not at all vulnerable to the sanctions of the law. He anticipates that Jessup will admit, as he testifies, that he did, indeed, order the Code Red and he is, indeed, proud of having done so.

At this point in the trial, and in Caffey's experience after graduation from Law School, he is confronted with a dilemma. He is a junior naval officer. If he attacks Colonel Jessup openly criticizing a senior he becomes vulnerable to being accused of the crime of subordination. On the other hand, as a lawyer, his duty is to do his best to defend his clients. The role of lawyer and the role of naval officer are clearly in conflict.

Caffee choses to act according to the values dictated by the lawyer role and in doing so comes to realize that *lawyering* is his natural work.

Jessup starts his testimony by claiming that he told Lieutenant Kendrick not to have his men administer a Code Red. He testifies that he told Markensen to have Santiago transferred. Caffey had noticed that Santiago's locker was filled with his personal belongings. He wonders out loud why Santiago was not packed if he was going to be flown to the States early the next morning. Caffey, who has examined the records of long distance calls from the base, also wonders out loud why Santiago made no calls to tell people he was coming home. These observations are the initial assault on the credibility of the Colonel.

Caffey continues by revealing a lack of logic at the core of the cover up. He asks Jessup whether or not his men always follow orders. The Colonel proudly responds that they do. "Have you ever served in an infantry unit? Put your life in another man's hands?" asks Jessup. "We follow orders or we die."

Caffey asks Jessup to reaffirm that he ordered Lieutenant Kendrick not to use the Code Red sanction. Jessup tells him that is true. Caffey asks Jessup to reaffirm that Kendrick did indeed order his men to refrain from the Code Red. Jessup tells him that is also true. Caffey wonders audibly why, if it is true that Marines always follow orders, and if it is true that there were orders not to give a Code Red, why is it that Dawson and Downey did use the Code Red on Santiago? He asks the rhetoric question, "If you gave an order that he was not to be touched, then why did he have to be transferred?" Colonel Jessup answers weakly, demonstrating the inconsistency of his former assertions, "Sometimes men take matters into their own hands."

"You snotty little bastard!" proclaims the Colonel, sneering at the attacking lawyer. The Colonel's complacency is starting to crumble. As this happens, Jessup falls back on his paramount source of strength, his professional pride, his expertise, his role of savior of American society. "You cant handle the truth," he says to the lawyer in front of the court martial jury. "We live in a world that has walls and those walls have to be guarded by men with guns. Santiago's death saved lives." "You want me on that wall!" the Colonel screams. "You need me on that wall!" he shouts. "I have neither the time nor the inclination to explain to a man who rises and sleeps in the blanket of the very freedom I provide and then questions the manner that I provide it. You're Goddamned dammed right! I did order the Code Red! I did my job! I would do it again!"

The Colonel has confessed to a crime. He is arrested. As a parting shot he says to Lawyer Caffey, "You have no idea how to defend a nation. You put peoples' lives in danger."

The way that we deal with the problem of role conflict, the way that we behave when we are conflicted by competing sets of values, reveals the nature of our authentic self. Role conflict results when we experience cognitive dissonance, mental stress caused by holding two or more contradictory beliefs, ideas, or values at the same time.

Leon Festingter's theory of cognitive dissonance focusses on how humans strive for internal consistency.[2] When dissonance is experienced, people are uncomfortable and will attempt to reduce dissonance and avoid situations that are likely to increase discomfort. It is in this manner that Sonny Steele chooses the role of *cowboy;* David chooses the role of *corporate executive;* Colonel Davenport chooses the role of *Father;* Caffey chooses the role of *lawyer.*

Paying attention to our behavior when we encounter role conflict and resolve the dissonance is one important aspect of living an examined life. Sensemaking theory reenforces this advice. Making sense out of the chaos of our daily lives does not result from explicitly delving into the deep recesses of our psyche or our soul, of being our own analyst. Observing the way we *behave* is much more feasible. Central to the idea of sensemaking is the tale of the little girl who is told to be sure of her meaning before she spoke. She responds with "How can I know what I think until I see what I say?" [3] Indeed, how can we be sure of what it is we are until we see what we do? David came to understand that *corporate employee* was his natural work as a result of him getting himself and Linda *Lost in America*. The same is true of Sonny Steele when he headed out of the casino aboard Rising Star and of Caffey when he decided to risk a Court Martial by destroying Colonel Jessup.

Chapter Fourteen

The Creative Rebel

Oh better far to live and die
Under the brave black flag I fly
Than play a sanctimonious part
With a pirate head and a pirate heart
Away to the cheating world go you
Where pirates all are well-to-do
But I'll be true to the song I sing
And live and die a Pirate King

The Pirates of Penzance, W.S.Gilbert

In the stories looked at so far we have seen examples of individuals avoiding or disobeying hierarchy and rules to satisfy their own values and aspirations. Rebelliousness, marching to the beat of one's own *drum* is part and parcel of the process of discovery one's authentic self. In *Twelve O'clock High* General Savage fakes radio failure so that he can avoid orders from headquarters to turn back due to problematic weather. He clings to the role of *leader*. He goes on to the target and develops pride in his subordinates. In the same story Major Stoval disobeys regulations when he delays the requests of aircrews to transfer out of the 918th Bomber Group. He assumes the role of *loyal subordinate*.

Jonathan in the *Rollerball* film refuses to retire when ordered to do so by Mr. Bartholomew. He maintains his roles of *athlete hero* and *teammate.* Sonny Steele in *Electric Horseman* breaks the law as he escapes the control of the corporation and flees aboard Rising Star. He seeks happiness by taking on the role of *cowboy.*

In the *A Few Good Men* story Lieutenant Caffey risks being charged with insubordination when he confronts Colonel Jessup. He embraces the role of *lawyer.*

When Karen Silkwood allows herself to become vulnerable to the invidious effect of radiation she steps into the role of *advocate for workers rights.* As we examine our own behavior and try to make sense out of that behavior, we can observe our own rebellion and that observation can tell us something about our authentic self.

Of course we need to listen to the beat of the *drum* of society and to the rules and constraints established by the hierarchy of our organization. Nevertheless, if we do this with absolute consistency and without ever questioning *the system* we run the risk of damage to our soul and to our happiness. This is what happened to Willie Kieth's father in the *Caine Mutiny* story and to Ivan Ilytch in Tolsoy's novel.

We need to reconcile the tension between the push of desire to achieve the rewards and satisfaction that comes from contributing to group effort and the pull of a quest to maintain the integrity of our own individuality. Such reconciliation must start with marching along a path toward a goal of self-understanding. Without this understanding there is no individuality to maintain. The organization tells you what to do to make a contribution to the system's effort. You are are trained and socialized to do exactly that. That is the easy part. The discovery of self, however, and the will to respond to the demands of that self is a much knottier proposition. You have to figure this out all by yourself. This takes time. It takes reflection. This means being willing at times to experiment by moving outside the boundaries of training and the restraints of socialization. This means being willing to eschew cooperation for defection.

Individual resistance to the dictates of organizational hierarchy does not necessarily result in degradation of the capacity of the organization to accomplish its mission. It is a paradox of organizational life that the modern organization needs the participation of people who are willing and able to *color outside the lines* of bureaucratic structure: rules, standard-ization, and obedience to hierarchy. If the organization could be perfectly designed to accomplish its intended purpose in all situations, there would be no necessity for any individual defection at all. Most organizational designs and strategies, however, are not perfect. The real world is just too complex and unpredictable to be captured by the design of an organized system. Because of this, disobedient behavior not only can help an individual discover and be true to the mandates of his or her own soul, it can help the organization achieve its goals.

Absolute executive control can be effective only when knowledge of the situation is complete and the organization can operate as a decision machine driving a fully analyzable system. Yet in the complex conditions that confront most modern and post modern organizations, the knowledge of the situation is incomplete and as a result the ability to predict with absolute certainty that decision *A* will produce result *B* is problematic. Systems of management control therefore can be hypotheses based on a manager's flawed conviction that his knowledge completely captures the realty of his organization's situation and enables him to predict the organization's future. The result is that as management attempts to control, it commits the analogy of a statistical type 2 error, i.e. accepting an hypothesis that is false. [1]

In the *Twelve O'clock High* narrative, General Savages's disobedience of the order to eschew going on to the target not only resulted in the short range accomplishment of the destruction of enemy assets, it also resulted in the long range improvement of the morale of the aircrews and their continuing willingness to risk their lives in the cause of the organization's mission.

When Sonny Steele stole the valuable equine property of the corporation this was a clear violation of the law. When Sonny's heroic and successful efforts to free Rising Star from the control of the corporation became exposed to public knowledge by way of TV, however, the sale of the corporations product of the corporation's product, Ranch Breakfast Cereal, increased dramatically. The publicity of Sonny's heroic behavior put the corporation in a favorable light. Sonny's defection became a corporation a benefit, one might even say a blessing in disguise.

Academic institutions are structured in accordance with bureaucratic prescriptions. Colleges have their Boards of Trustees, Provosts, Deans, and Departmental Chairpersons. College policy and rules are specified in lengthy detailed Faculty Handbooks. At the same time institutions of higher learning hold sacred the principle of *academic freedom.* Professors are constrained by management control *and at the some time* allowed, indeed encouraged, to express the originality, imagination, and individuality required by their teaching and research roles. Without this capacity to exercise professional wiggle room the process of higher education would be a useless hollow shell. Academic managers want to exercise control over the faculty. At the same time they need to loosen that control if the organization's mission is to be accomplished.

Looking back on my own experience as a career professional naval officer brings to mind how even in a military organization where discipline and conformity are core values, the requirement for the exercise of individual discretion is recognized in one way or another. My indoctrination as a midshipman student at the U.S.Naval Academy in Annapolis included exposure to the notion that you rate, i.e. deserve, anything you can get away with. On the one hand I was told to obey and that dishonesty was a cardinal sin. On the other hand there was the contradictory clearly stated suggestion that failing to obey might be acceptable, even desired, as long as you were clever enough to get away with defection. The unstated assumption behind this seemingly contradictory guidance was that your dedication and professionalism would constrain you to practice defection only when the defection resulted in the greater good.

There is hidden genius in a Naval Academy tradition which recognizes the usefulness of individual discretion to the organized system and the danger of unquestioning obedience to formal mandates. My experience as a student at the Academy included strongly expressed displays of school spirit when football games were scheduled. This was particularly true during the week preceding the annual Army-Navy football game. At mealtimes, midshipmen would rise, one table at a time, and shout, "BEAT ARMY." Once this wave got started, at every other table the midshipmen bleated out, "BEAT THE SYSTEM." Here at the shrine of naval profession- alism, the birthplace of admirals, the temple of orderliness and discipline, midshipmen joyously expressed not only their quest for the defeat of the Army football team, but with equal enthusiasm they proclaimed an inspi- ration to beat the SYSTEM!

Of course, the phenomenon of rebellious creativity involves the mat- ters of ethics and morality. The distinction between what is ethical and moral and what is not depends on the capacity to recognize the differ- ence between what helps the organized system and what damages the system. The matter of morality and ethics will be explored in a subse- quent chapter. For now, let's examine the phenomenon of individual dis- cretion and defection and the way that this plays out.

Chapter Fifteen

The Start of a Work in Progress

Can'st follow the track of the dolphin
Or tell where the sea swallows roam;
Where leviathan taketh his pastime;
What ocean he calleth his home?
Even so with the words of thy seniors,
And the orders those words shall convey.
Every law is as naught beside this one-
"Thou shalt not criticize, but obey!"

From The Laws of the Navy

The motivation to respond to the call of your inner self by failing to obey the dictates or norms of an organization often comes as a result of a moment of sudden revelation or insight. Sonny Steele's decision to flee with the stallion Rising Star, for example, was the result of his unanticipated and painful identification with an animal that has become a tool of the corporation. My own initiation into the process of defection, an event that encouraged me to take the first step on a road that might lead to the discovery of my unique individual self, came about very early in my naval career.

My life after graduation and commissioning as an Ensign in the U.S. Navy started with assignment to flight school. After a year and a half of training I was awarded the coveted navy wings of gold and designated a naval aviator.

My aircraft squadron flew the Neptune P2V aircraft. I had my eye on this particular airplane since midshipman days. First of all, the plane had a crew of nine. I am a people oriented person and the thought of flying around in a lonely cockpit of one did not appeal to me. Of course, single seat aircraft do their "thing" in groups of formations and that surely is teamwork. My own concept of teamwork, however, was a bunch of guys sitting in the same plane directly coordinating their talents to achieve a common goal, in this case flying over the ocean for long periods of time, keeping track of Soviet submarines as well as their surface ships and conducting surveillance of the merchant ships of all nations. A bit later these sorts of planes were to be instrumental in tracking communist bloc ships that were transporting missiles to Cuba, missiles that produced the famous 1962 crisis.

The P2V aircraft was appealing to me because it was a safe plane, at least much safer than some of the other choices I might have made. At this point in my young life, I had no desire to challenge fate by joining what seemed to me to be the daredevils of naval aviation who fly on and off Aircraft Carriers. This experience would come later.

The P2V had an almost perfect safety record. She had four engines, two powerful reciprocating motors that drove large propellers and two small jets. The jets had been added on to allow the plane to take off at the much heavier weights which resulted from the adding on of increasing numbers of electronic black boxes designed to improve submarine hunting ability. The jets were used for takeoff and immediately shut down once airborne. Using the jets constantly would burn precious fuel and reduce the advantage of long range cruising and searching capability.

That was another thing that appealed to me about the P2V. It had great range, long legs. It could be used to go far away places. The idea of having breakfast in Florida and lunch in Bermuda was very appealing. The idea of spending a week in frigid Newfoundland and then a month in sunny Puerto Rico satisfied the promise of the recruiting slogan, "Join the Navy and See the World."

My assignment to the aircraft squadron was for four years, 1959-1962. I served first as navigator and copilot and later as pilot-in-charge as the squadron deployed from its Florida base to more or less exotic places like Sicily and some not so exotic places like Iceland and Greenland. My ground job was as personnel officer and later as operations scheduling officer. Things were working out very well. The radio call sign for squadron aircraft was "Spangle." That seemed to fit. My life as a naval aviator was shining brightly.

Every squadron has one officer assigned to the job of Safety Officer. His task is to conduct and supervise programs of accident prevention. The job also involves investigating aircraft accidents and incidents (near accidents). These investigations were for the purpose of revealing weaknesses in people, material, and procedure. Lessons learned would improve safety by preventing future accidents.

The incumbent Safety Officer in my P2V squadron, a Lieutenant Commander, considerably senior to me, was not a busy man. The P2V was an inherently safe aircraft. It was, nevertheless, a requirement that the squadron have a Safety Officer and this fellow busied himself with the creation of posters broadcasting trite slogans like "Complacency Kills!" and "Plan the Flight, Fly the Plan" and sitting in his office reading paper backs with pictures on the cover that were quite sexy, at least by the standards of that era.

One day orders for the Lieutenant Commander to transfer to another duty station arrived. For some reason he was scheduled to depart a few weeks before the arrival of his replacement. The squadron could not be without someone filling this job, if only to satisfy a formal procedural requirement. Accordingly I was notified by my commanding officer that effective immediately I would, even as a lieutenant (junior grade at that), be the safety officer, at least until the arrival of the replacement for the departing Lieutenant Commander.

"What do I have to do?", I inquired.

"Nothing except occupy the Safety Office," I was told.

So I occupied the closet sized one-man office. It was not a bad job. Some of the time I flew assigned missions, mostly patrolling the Atlantic waters off the Florida coast. The rest of the time I sat in the Safety Office reading the paperback novels of Mickey Spillane that stocked the draws of the beat up ancient desk that was to be my lonely perch for the next few weeks.

Then it happened! The squadron duty officer, his face as white as snow, burst into the office. "Spangle Twelve is down near Naval Air Station Brunswick, Georgia."

I requested that a plane be readied for me to fly to Brunswick, only about a twenty minute flight from Jacksonville. As I approached the airfield I could see a smoldering mass of the remains of a charred P2V about three miles from the end of the active runway. I landed and was driven out to the sight of the crash. The air was filled with the odor of burning fuel, oil, and human flesh. Immersed in the still burning wreckage of the airplane were the charred dead bodies of seven of my squadron mates. I was ordered to remain on site until the arrival of four members of my squadron who, along with me, were appointed as the investigation board. The board was led by our squadron Operations Officer, a Commander... very senior to me and to the other officers.

The investigation started the following morning. It was not very difficult to determine the direct cause of the accident. The crew of two officers and five enlisted technicians were on a daylight clear-weather training mission. They had flown from Jacksonville to the airfield at Brunswick to practice simulated bad weather ground radar controlled approaches. This was a standard training event.

The cockpit crew consisted of a pilot, copilot, and enlisted plane captain who sat between these two and handled various duties such as monitoring engine performance and managing the control of fuel from various tanks to the airplane's engines. When approaching the runway in response to a ground based radar operator's instructions, in position to land at about 100 feet of altitude, the crew would level off, climb, and start another practice approach. Throughout this entire process the cockpit crew would be in radio contact with the radar controller on the ground. On one approach the transmit button on the cockpit radio mike stuck. Every sound in the cockpit was broadcast and the transmissions, in accordance with standard operating procedure, were recorded.

On the fatal pass, as the pilot added power to go around the right engine started belching black smoke. The pilot ordered that the engine be shut down by the flight engineer and that fuel to that engine be shut off by turning off a fuel flow valve. Shortly thereafter the recorded voice of the pilot informed the people on the ground that "Spangle Twelve is going in." That was the end of Spangle Twelve and its crew.

The first step in the investigation was to get witness statements. The most important of these was from the tower operator who confirmed that it was the right engine of the plane that was smoking. The next steps were to gather up the destroyed parts of the aircraft, to reconstruct the plane as much as possible, and in this way search for clues revealing the cause of the accident.

Before long it was clear that with the right engine malfunctioning and probably on fire the cockpit crew, most likely either the copilot or the plane captain, shut down the (healthy) left engine. It was also clear that the fuel control valve to the right engine had been closed, probably by the plane captain. The left engine had been shut down and its propeller feathered, blades rotated so as to stop the revolution of the propeller, and the right engine had been shut down by starving it from fuel flow.

Once the nitty-gritty work of investigation was complete, the members of the accident investigation board convened in a small conference room. Our task was to write up the accident report. This was to be a very detailed description of our findings as well an offering of our recommendations. The findings that dealt with the direct cause of the accident were cut and dried. The cockpit crew in a rush to deal with the smoking engine shut down both engines. This was a case of engine malfunction compounded by "pilot error!" That was it.

The direct cause of the accident was clear. There was however more to the investigation than this determination. In addition to direct causes, the board must make judgments and recommendations concerning contributing causes. These might be such things as weather conditions, fatigue, training shortfalls, unsuitable standard operating procedures, etc. Rarely is an accident the result of only one single cause. Most are caused by a complex chain of events: a part that is poorly designed and therefore can be installed improperly, the failure of a technical system when the part is not properly installed, the inability of the pilot to deal with the situation, poor weather conditions that prevent a successful emergency landing etc. etc. etc. A thorough investigation uncovers all of the links in such a chain of events and in this way complete understanding leads to lessons learned.

In this accident, there were two possibilities of including significant "contributing" causes in the investigation report. Squadron training records indicated that the plane captain had not competed a full course of required training in emergency procedures. The squadron was short of plane captains on the day of the flight so this unfortunate lad was assigned to fill in. There were also some questions concerning the documented training of the pilot-in-command of this fatal flight. His training was probably complete, but you could not prove this by looking at the written record.

A second possible contributing factor had to do with standard operating procedures. The two auxiliary jet engines were only operated for approaches and landings in poor weather. The usefulness of these engines idling during approaches in poor weather was that if there was a problem with a main, propeller driven, engine the pilot might have more than he could handle, what with the weather and other problems. So the jets were started and could be used at any time to help out if there were a problem. In the case of this particular flight, however, the jets were turned off in accordance with standard procedure because the weather was clear. I believed that had the jets been running when the propeller engine started to belch smoke the cockpit crew would have been under less stress because they would have had two extra engines available.

When it came time to write up the accident investigation report I suggested that we include weaknesses in the plane captain training program and in the pilot training documentation as contributing causes. I also suggested that we recommend that from now on the jet engines be started prior to commencing an approach to landing in any weather.

The Commander who was the senior investigating officer rejected both of my suggestions out of hand. "If we find fault in the training process the squadron Commanding Officer would be held accountable," the Commander said. "His career would be ruined." Moreover, I was told that it was silly to have the jets going for every landing. That would be a waste of fuel and anyway a pilot should be able to handle any situation without the help of extra engines.

I tried to convince the board members that the lesson learned concerning the importance of training was more important than any political fallout from our report. I also made the point that if the jets of Spangle Twelve had been running during these clear weather practice approaches this accident probably would not have happened. My fellow junior officers were willing to sign the report without including my thoughts concerning contributing factors. I was not willing to sign and I could not be ordered to sign. Perhaps the sound of Midshipmen proclaiming the desire, even the necessity, to "Beat the System" during college days was echoing in my mind. More likely, my sensitivity to human pain and my personality as a people oriented person encouraged me to resist any cover up of even indirect causes of the tragic accident. For whatever reason, I took the situation personally (just as Sonny Steel took the situation of Rising Star personally).

For five days the accident investigation board continued to meet. Our meals were brought to us in an improvised meeting room at the Air Station. For five days we all starred at each other. The Commander's stare was more of a glare. Finally, at the end of the fifth day our senior member gave in and the others followed. There were no words offered by him. He merely reached across the table for the pages containing the paragraphs I had prepared concerning contributing causes and recommendations.

He then checked the relevant boxes on the relevant form: weaknesses in training, weaknesses in standard procedures. He signed the report. The junior officers, including myself, added their signatures.

Our squadron commanding officer was neither reprimanded nor punished. He went on to a successful, if not spectacular, career. Higher authority rejected the recommendation concerning the use of jets in clear weather landings.

The trauma of Spangle Twelve never left my mind. This whole mess had a profound cognitive and emotional effect on me. My perception of the P2V as a plane that would never crash was destroyed. The sight of the smoldering bodies of my squadron mates was devastating. What had been a shining spangle previously was now a tragic and bleak cloud of fear, anger, and doubt. I had not slept at all since the accident. Through this fog of pain, however, one thing was perfectly clear. I was not going to sign the report unless the contributing factors that the commander had rejected were included. [1]

A few years later, I ran into the senior officer that I had confronted during the accident investigation. It was a chance meeting at an overseas officer's club. We did not talk for long. Yet for me there was at least some closure when he reminisced about the Spangle Twelve accident. "You were right," he said. " And I respect you for that." Then he did the strangest thing. He saluted me. I believed, and still do, that his salute was a recognition of the way that my professionalism dominated the political factors that were part and parcel of our organization as a bureaucratic system.

The impact of all this on my journey of self discover was an acceptance of the mandate that professionalism on occasion must trump the power of hierarchy. This edict formed a frame of reference which helped me make sense of the remaining years of my career.

Of course, I did not have any conception of a definition or a concept of professionalism or bureaucracy per se at the time. Sitting here writing this as a student and teacher of social and political science at this stage of my life, however, enables me to explain what I now understand to be the meaning of my experience. Formal definitions of concepts or the complications of theory notwithstanding, my paying attention to own behavior helped me to make sense out of this tragic event and to be influenced by that sensemaking for the rest of my career.

Looking back on those days, and trying to explain to readers and myself my reaction to events it becomes clear to me that my own behavior revealed to me an aspect of my authentic self. Remember the sensemaking notion, "Don't as me what I think until I see what I say." What I have said here makes it evident to me that the road to my own self understanding and happiness was paved with the *mortar* of self examination.

Chapter Sixteen

The Risk and the Rewards

Many people wait throughout their whole lives for the chance to be good in their own fashion

Nietche

The important distinction between bureaucracy and professionalism must have been implicitly implanted in my psyche early in my days as a Midshipman at the Naval Academy. First came the demonstration of the fact that the bureaucratic impulse rests on the notion of hierarchy and the distribution of top to bottom power.

My first I exposure to the the law of obedience came in the form of the gold insignia on the collar of a newly commissioned Ensign. He was assigned to guide our early indoctrination and organizational socialization, to encourage us to surrender our individual selves and become uniform parts of a *well oiled system*.

I was given the opportunity to volunteer for one form or another of athletic activity. Here I would compete with other companies of plebes (i.e. freshmen) and learn an important lesson for future Navy professionals, the importance of winning. As a city boy who had played basketball, football, and baseball in high school, I was fascinated with the idea of doing something different, something high class, something like rowing on a team of eight that propelled sleek fragile wooden boats, shells, down the Severn River in exhausting races. I volunteered for the sport of crew.

The leader of my company was a newly graduated Ensign, assigned to stay on for the summer to manage the initial indoctrination of us future naval officers. Our Ensign's own dedication to winning was an example for us all. He had one problem, at least one that I know of. His company boxing team lacked a heavyweight. My own weight was plenty heavy and I had boxed as a youngster in summer camp. Our Ensign informed me that I should forget the sport of crew and sign on as the heavyweight member of the company boxing team. I assumed that the word *volunteer*, as it applied to choosing a sport, was meant literally. I assumed that I had the discretion to pick and choose the venue for the spilling of my sweat in the cause of glory. In some respects I was right. In some respects I was wrong. I informed my Ensign that I was volunteering for crew. He didn't seem happy about this. I didn't think his unhappiness was relevant to my situation.

As part of our marching activity, we would undergo daily rifle inspection. Each day we spent many hours disassembling and cleaning our nearly antique M-1 rifles. Mine was spotless, inside and out. So were the rifles of all my peers. I believed that the teaching point here was that if we expected a weapon to take care of us in combat, we needed to take care of the weapon. That turned out not to be the teaching point.

On the day following my insistence on volunteering for the crew team, as we stood at "inspection arms" our Ensign walked down the ranks, rapidly snatching the rifle from the hands of each midshipman, quickly glancing at the external condition of the weapon, holding the barrel to his eye, allowing daylight to flow from the muzzle to the chamber, searching for any spot of dirt. As he held up my rifle in this manner, he exclaimed, "This is filthy!" I was aghast and he could see that I was. "Here," he said, "Look for yourself."

I looked at the lining of the rifle barrel and it shone with pristine brilliance. "It's clean, sir," I proclaimed.

"It's filthy," he responded, the sparkling brand new gold bars high-lighting the starched collar of his khaki uniform. He followed this with the assignment of an appropriate number of demerits and, more important, with punishment consisting of a considerable number of hours of march-ing off extra duty in my practically nonexistent spare time.

It was from this ensign that I learned the *Golden Rule of Hierarchy*: "He who has the gold, makes the rule!" [1]

So much for the demonstration of the way that the power of the hi-erarchy influences outcomes. This step on my journey put me into the position of a battle between my inner self, the self that wanted to have my own way, and the practicality of my circumstance, the demand for un-questioned obedience and the consequences of failure to obey. The way I adapted to this uncomfortable situation was telling my self that *they* have control of my body, but not of my mind. Of course, I did not have much of an idea of exactly what it indeed was I had on my mind, yet I did know it was not absolute unquestioning obedience. At the time I had no idea that the *Golden Rule* might have a negative impact on my capacity to be true to myself, whatever myself was. The realization that the discovery of one's authentic self and the development of the will to be true to that self can result only from long term examination of the sign posts of experience along life's journey.

My early exposure to the *Golden Rule of Hierarchy* did make it clear that there was more than one purpose to my organization. My purpose, in this instance, was participating in the sport of rowing. The Ensign's pur-pose was bringing about the absolute compliance of subordinates so as to train and socialize them to eschew personal needs and desires and thereby help the organization to maintain its viability and capability. Much later I experienced the same phenomenon when the senior member of the accident board pushed for protecting the reputation of our Commanding Officer. He was responding to the organizational purpose of maintaining the well-being of the system. The Commanding Officer represents the image of the squadron as a whole. Damage to him meant damage to the squadron as a whole. These impulses are the same that we have seen in the behavior of General Pritchard in *Twelve O'clock* High story. Pritchard wanted to push on with risky and experimental daylight precision bombing because he desired to maintain the robustness of the Army Air Force as a viable organization.

Chapter Seventeen

The Quest for Absolute Control

In order to act wisely, it is not enough to be wise

Dostoevski

The point has been made (in chapter fourteen) that effective absolute executive control can be achieved only when knowledge of the situation is complete and the organization can operate as a decision machine driving a fully analyzable system. Yet in the complex conditions that confront most modern and post modern organizations, the knowledge of the situation, is incomplete and as a result the ability to predict with absolute certainty that decision *A* will produce result *B* is problematic.

The quest for effective leadership, i.e. control of human behavior and production of desired results, often requires decision making in conditions of complexity and uncertainty. In an attempt to deal with more complexity and uncertainty than the human mind can reliably deal with leaders have come increasingly to rely on the use of computers to gather, store, manipulate, and analyze data. The underlying assumption is that human understanding of complex situations is limited because the human mind cannot gather store and understand the vast amount of information that fully describes a complex situation. The machine can thereby become the manifestation of bureaucratic structure when it is programed with standard procedures (rules), the capacity to compartmentalize diverse functions (division of labor) and to produce commands that can direct and evaluate human activity (hierarchy).

As computers become the engines of modern management there is pressure for the lower level participant to consider the necessity to exercise individual discretion and the requirement to push against in invidious impact of machine driven bureaucracy by being true to professional norms. If the computer is the replica of the managing bureaucrat and professional norms are antithetical to the norms of bureaucracy as a form of organizing then we may expect that the professional will push against the computer just as he or she might push against the managing bureaucrat.

It is clear that humans are imperfect beings when it comes to the absolute understanding of the mysteries the post modern era as chaos seems to be the order of the day. It should come as no surprise, therefore, that we find it useful, even rational, to create and use artificial systems like the computers in an attempt to overcome human shortfalls. This makes a great deal of sense out of Phil's enlightenment, in the *Groundhog Day* story, when he proposes that "Only God knows everything." More appropriate today, Phil might have said that in the age of computers in general and artificial intelligence in particular "The computer knows everything!"

The confrontation between man and machine is illuminated by the story told in the film *2001, A Space Odyssey.*[1] This movie tells the tale of a group of astronauts sent from earth to Jupiter on an important mission. There is a good possibility that intelligent life exits on that planet and the crew of the spaceship has been sent to explore the possibility. The executive decision maker on board is an advanced computer named HAL. HAL has been programmed, i.e. trained, to navigate the spaceship to its destination and to solve problems that may be encountered on the journey. HAL has also been programmed to learn. He (perhaps I should say *it*) can modify mechanical *thinking* as HAL confronts situations that are not anticipated by those who designed the original program. HAL's thinking may be artificial, but it is not set in concrete.

All of the programming, the personality, of HAL has been skewed in accordance with the value oriented criteria that mission accomplishment is the highest priority of all. The decision making criteria of the computer is consistent with the values that influence General Savage, Mr. Bartholomew, the head of the accident investigation board, the Ensign in charge of my company at the Naval Academy... leaders and managers described in the cases and stories discussed so far.

During the flight toward Jupiter HAL decides to take over the spaceship, to mutiny by manipulating the life support equipment in a manner that kills the ship's human crew. This draconian motivation of the machine is driven by the program which infuses the computer with: the priority of mission accomplishment, the assumption that computer decision making is error free, and that human decision making is error prone. If humans are fallible and the hierarchy programed into the machine is not, it might be best to eliminate error by eliminating human influence.

This is the same way that the human bureaucratic organism is *programmed*. The human bureaucratic organizational structure is based on the presumption that person at the top of a hierarchy is more capable of making efficacious decisions than lower level participants. The fundamental unstated assumption is that the boss knows best.

From the point of view of the computer in this story, the probability of mission success will be enhanced if the human crew is destroyed and the computer takes over. The focus of the film's drama is the battle of wits in a life and death struggle between HAL and the last remaining live human on board, Dave.

The confrontation between HAL and Dave is analogous to the confrontations we have examined in the cases described as individuals pursue the quest to discover their authentic individuality. In my own experience as a naval officer I came dramatically face to face with a mechanical computer-bureaucrat. This experience, not all that different from Dave's conflict with HAL, brought me one step closer to understanding the nature of my authentic self.

During my tour of duty aboard the aircraft carrier U.S.S. Lexington we sailed to Boston for a periodic overhaul. The overhaul was to be accomplished over a period of seven months and would result in major maintenance and upgrading of all aspects of the ship and its operating systems. The work was to be done by members of the ship's crew and by a civilian workforce of unionized employees. Traditionally, these overhauls would be completed as each shipboard department worked in fairly intimate contact with a functional counterpart of the civilian shipyard.

Experienced officers, which by now included me, knew that civilian workers who were not a formal part of the ship's hierarchy could not be controlled effectively with an authoritarian style of leadership. The *Golden Rule of Hierarchy* simply was not at all acceptable to them. This was because the unionized civilian employees were responsible to the shipyard and not directly to the ship and because as highly skilled laborers they resented being pushed around by officers. Blue collar workers considered officers to be dilettantes. Moreover, union membership did give the workers a good deal of potential power of their own.

An informal relationship between ship's officers and civilian workers had been traditionally established in order to accomplish an effective overhaul. This relationship was achieved by the time honored prescription of, " You scratch my back and I'll scratch yours." On the part of the ship's crew this meant giving the civilian shipyard workers much leeway in deciding the day to day work schedule and procedures as well as giving them unauthorized *side payments* such as large bags of coffee that were always available in the ship's store of consumables, and free meals in the enlisted mess. On the part of the civilian workers this meant doing whatever had to be done to produce the desired result of the overhaul, including the maintenance and installation of equipment and the performance of work that was desired by the crew, but not necessarily part of the formally authorized overhaul package and budget.

Managerial supervision and coordination of the overhaul was traditionally accomplished by a group of naval officer-engineers organized into a project team titled "Supervisor of Ship Construction and Repair" and known as "Supship". The "Supship" team consisted of just a few officers and these could not keep up with the thousands of details of the overhaul of an aircraft carrier. Because of this, and because of the impossibility of integrating the civilian shipyard workers into a military hierarchy, supervision on the part of "Supship" was traditionally loose. In the past, the details of the overhaul had not been centrally controlled.

This particular overhaul for the U.S.S. Lexington was to be different. In response to a general trend toward the latest version of scientific management, higher naval authority in Washington had decided to use a computer assisted management information system that could be applied to the overhaul of an Aircraft Carrier. The system was called "Ship's Force Overhaul Management System" [SFOMS]. The intent of SFOMS was to control the utilization of the ship's crew and shipyard workforce activity in a way that would provide for the efficient accomplishment of the overhaul. Equipment was considered to be a fixed cost and man-hours were therefore perceived to be the limiting factor controlling efficiency. SFOMS was to rationally divide the necessary man-hours among the ship's crew and the shipyard work force components and to monitor achievement.

For one year prior to the overhaul all ship departments were required to identify each necessary shipyard job. The details of each job, ranging in complexity from replacing light bulbs and the filters on electronic equipment to replacing the entire flight deck and its catapult and airplane landing arresting equipment, were made part of a comprehensive computer program. The program included weekly progress checks based on a comparison of man-hours estimated for the job completion and actual accomplishment. Daily computer inputs on punch cards were to be generated on the job so as to keep the computer up to date with the reality of progress. Each week the computer would spit out a report that would inform the ship's Commanding Officer, the shipyard Commanding Officer, and each shipboard Department Head concerning whether or not a Department was on schedule, ahead of schedule or behind schedule.

If the old system of cooperation between civilian workers and the navy people did not involve a *Golden Rule of Hierarchy*, the new SFOMS system would. The computer had the *Gold* (the information), and it would *Rule*. Now, it would be the computer that gave the orders, supervised the work, and evaluated the results. The old system merely got the job done. The new system was designed to get the job done with a perfection of efficiency hitherto unimagined, a perfection of efficiency that could not possibly be achieved by human effort and interacion.

As the Department Head of the Communications Department I was responsible for the maintenance and operation of a vast array of sophisticated communications equipment including receivers, transmitters, teletype machines and electronic cryptographic equipment. During this overhaul virtually all communications equipment would be replaced or upgraded. The overhaul of the living spaces for communications personnel was also scheduled.

Communications was a unique shipboard department. My seniors on the ship, the Commanding Officer and Executive Officer had little or no expertise vis-a-vis the communications function. I had little enough myself. I depended on a group of highly trained dedicated technical people.

Cryptographic procedures that subsumed just about all communications called for tight security. This gave me the opportunity to operate my department free of any detailed supervision by my superiors in the hierarchy. My bosses had *no* direct knowledge of anything that I did. As long as the ship was able to perform required communications functions, nobody seemed to care what I was doing. I liked this discretion because it enabled me to trust my subordinate specialists and to convince them that the only thing that really mattered was results.

It was clear that the use of the SFOMS management control system was designed to minimize departmental discretion. The esoteric nature of my job, however, enabled me to escape from the omnipresent eye of the computer and its threatening reports on progress.

Prior to entering the shipyard I noticed that my technical work force frequently had to work around official procedures in order to get the job done. This meant "jury rigging" circuits and equipment as well as taking various procedural and administrative short cuts. I looked the other way at appropriate moments and from time to time told little white lies to my superiors, falsehoods concerning the status of various equipments and procedures. I did not want my seniors to become involved in "micro-managing" the communications functions. This did not create any problems. I was left alone and received only the most general guidance from above. I provided only the most general guidance to my subordinates. The department operated virtually free of direct supervision and free of problems. We got the job done.

As we entered the shipyard I perceived the SFOMS management information system as a threat to the effectiveness of my department. I did not like the idea of a computer looking over my shoulder and forcing me to look over the shoulders of my technical expert subordinates. I was concerned that the paper work required to feed the computer would rob my people of the precious time that was required to get the overhaul work done. I knew that the SFOMS, if taken seriously, would preclude the sort of "you scratch my back I'll scratch yours" relationship between my people and the shipyard electronics division, a relationship that was necessary to accomplish an effective overhaul.

With all this alarming baggage burdening me, I formulated a scheme to implement SFOMS in a way that might counteract what I knew to be its dysfunctional impact. First, I set aside a small room that would be used exclusively to prepare daily punch cards for the computer. Then I trained one of my smartest and most loyal junior enlisted men in the administrative procedures required by SFOMS. Once the overhaul period commenced, this fine lad would run the entire overhaul for the Communications Department *as a simulation.* My man would check to see what the "program" called for on any given day and proceed to punch cards in a manner appropriate to having fulfilled the expectations of the computer. In this manner the department, according to the computer generated output, was always exactly where it was supposed to be with respect to daily progress and man hour utilization.

At the weekly shipyard progress meetings all departments except the Communications Department were chided for being behind the SFOMS specified schedule. Various excuses were made, including the irrationality of the program itself. The Communications Department was always mentioned as a model of effective management.

I kept in close touch with the shipyard civilian electronic workers. I made sure that they were kept happy and were provided with the traditional unauthorized *side payment* bribes. The shipyard workers responded positively. By the end of the seven month period all communications equipment had been overhauled or replaced. Some new equipment that was previously unexpected had mysteriously arrived and been installed. All Communications living spaces had been painted and made otherwise more attractive and livable. The other departments were not nearly as successful.

Shipyard workers assigned to jobs replacing flight deck equipment, an Air Department responsibility, had gone on strike three months into the overhaul period to protest working conditions and procedures that were outside of contract provisions. By the time the strike was settled the overhaul had been delayed for two months and the yard period had to be extended accordingly.

At the four month mark a fire broke out in the engine room below decks as a result of shipyard worker carelessness when doing a welding job. Damage was estimated at three million dollars.

I am not sure exactly why I had to cheat to get the job done. Probably because the rules of the game, the SFOMS game, did not fit the knotty complications of reality. More important, I'm not sure why I was willing to take a big risk to get the job at hand done. I do remember, however, that of the many euphemisms planted in my mind back in Annapolis days, this one applied to the shipyard situation. *You rate anything you can get away with.* Of course, there was an honor code and the code simply prohibited lying, cheating and stealing. Given this ethic, how might the notion that you deserve what you get away with make sense? The answer, I think, has to do with the near worship of pragmatism and its relationship to the profession of arms. A lawyer friend of mine once told me that "Winning isn't the only thing, it is EVERYTHING." Now if that has any relevance to the legal profession and its ethics, it has the world of relevance to the fighting person. In a war, tragically enough, when the dust settles it is the victors that get not only the spoils, but also the absolution from sin. When was the last time you heard about a winner being accused of a war crime? It is the losers that suffer in this way.

My cheating the computer was certainly not a crime against humanity. I did, however, take a personal risk. The willingness to take a risk, to put your behind on the line is a strong norm of the naval profession. What would have happened if I were caught? Could I have been able to defend myself? Of course not. That would have put me in the category of "sea lawyer," that vile lower than human form of life who tries to make excuses. The only proper answer to the question, "Why did you disobey?" an answer that echoes to me from Midshipman days, is "No Excuse, Sir."

The unqualified distinction between — (1) the requirement that we need to have the discretion to cheat the system for our own sake and/or for the sake of the system and (2) if you get caught marching to the beat of your own drummer you will be punished— presents us with the temptation to see the distinction between what is right and what is wrong as a multiple choice quiz. Life in general, however, and life as a member of an organization in particular, is much more complicated than can be conceived of in *black* or *white* colors. Responding to the authority of our authentic self and thereby becoming the author of our own story requires more than dealing with multiple choice questions. It requires more in the way of an essay, or even a book, the pages of which span the decades of your experience in the world of work.

Chapter Eighteen

Morality and Ethics

*...Responsibility can no longer be looked upon as merely
a response for executing polices already formulated.
We have to face the fact that responsibility is much more
comprehensive in scope.*

Cal Friedrich

*You've got to be taught
To hate and fear,
You've got to be taught
From year to year,
It's got to be drummed
In your dear little ear
You've got to be carefully taught.*

The play South Pacific Oscar Hamerstein

*There can be no happiness if the things we believe in are
different from the things we do*

Freya Stark

As a we decide to respond to the call of our authentic self when that call
comes into conflict with the demands of the powers that be we take on

a weighty responsibility. The consequences of our behavior, for better or worse, for good or evil, will rest on our own shoulders and we can be held accountable for those consequences. The push of responsibility comes from within ourselves. The pull of accountability comes from the hierarchy of the organization. Our happiness depends the way we deal with the desire to do the right thing and the requirement to serve the purpose of our organization when these demands clash.

In the *Twelve O'clock High* story Colonel Davenport assumes responsibility for the survival of the aircrews of the 918th Bomber Group. The organization, under the command of General Pritchard, needs to place the airmen in a situation where they will almost certainly die. Pritchard holds Davenport accountable for his attitude and behavior. He fires him.

When Karen Silkwood decided to take responsibility for the safety of workers she died.

As we listen to Socrates and try to live an examined life we come closer to understanding the purpose that is spawned by our authentic self. When Sonny Steele observed the status of the stallion Rising Star as a flunky of the organization, the purpose of his own soul was revealed. Colonel Davenport, Sonny Steele, and myself as well as I came face to face with computer assisted management control, all wanted to do the *right* thing, the virtuous *thing*. What, indeed *is* the *thing* that is right? How does the decision to do *right* push us toward or away from our journey along the path of self understanding and living a life worth living?

When we think about the desire to do the right thing, the matters of ethics and morality come to mind. We often conceive of ethics and morality as equivalent concepts. There is, however, a significant difference between the criterion of ethics and those of morality. This difference is relevant to the desire to do the *right* thing as we take responsibility for our behavior as a member of an organization or for that matter as a human element of society in general.

Codes of ethics per se are devised by the hierarchy of organizations or by those who specify professional decision criteria. In this respect they are external to the individual and are usually closely related to the purposes of an organization or a profession. General Savage's behavior is motivated by the ethic of sacrifice when he tells his aircrews that "We are in a war, a fighting war, and some of us are going to *have* to die." He advises his men to accept this code by "considering themselves already dead." The ethic of sacrifice, even the ultimate sacrifice, is codified by the oath that the airmen have taken to "Support and defend the Constitution of the United States against all enemies, foreign and domestic" and furthermore that this oath is taken "without any mental reservation or purpose of evasion."

Physicians, when they are certified with the MD degree, take an oath that they will "First of all, do no harm." It may be unrealistic to expect the airmen to consider themselves "already dead" or to expect that the physician will ply his profession with absolute perfection and *never* do any harm. Nevertheless, the matter of doing the *right* thing conceived of as the *ethical* thing takes the form of a prescribed code that is mandated by considerations that are external to the individual and may not conform to the unique situation or nature, i.e. authentic self, of the individual.

As we comply with the ethics mandates of our organization we accept and work toward the accomplishment of organizational purpose. Usually this does not involve a conflict with the values that make up the role specified by our authentic self. At times, however, push can come to shove and that is when the ethical constraints of the system come into conflict with the moral structure of our individuality. This was the case when the senior member of the accident investigation board I was a member of insisted that I avoid documenting causes that reflect negatively on our squadron Commanding Officer. The ethics of the organization concerning the status of senior officers is reflected in a stanza of the poem titled *Laws of the Navy* that I was required to memorize and spout out as a Plebe (freshman) at the Naval Academy.

> Take heed what you say of your seniors
> Be the word spoken softly or plain
> Lest the bird of the air tell the matter
> And then ye shall hear it again

The relevant distinction between ethics and morality is that the former is generated by what is external to the individual and the later is a critical element of the individual's authentic self.

The ideas of the psychologist Abraham Maslow[1] and the those of Socrates as expressed by Plato more than 2000 years earlier tell us in one way or another that to trod along the path to self understanding and happiness the inner voice which is the source of our morality should at times trump the edict of organizationally imposed norms, i.e. ethics.

Let's start with Maslow. Maslow's subject was motivation, explanations for why we do what we do. His theory of human motivation is taught in courses that teach students how to understand human motivation and how to use that understanding to encourage subordinates to perform their duties with dependability, dedication, and energy. These same ideas, however, can be used to help us understand our own motivation and to use that understanding to become aware of the connection between our individual morality, the source of which is our authentic self, and our happiness.

Abraham Maslow, tells us that human needs can best be understood in terms of a hierarchy ranging from survival, to associational, to self esteem, to self-actualization. Lower level needs, at the first step on Maslow's hierarchy, tend to be held in common by all human beings. We all need food, shelter, and safety. Without these security needs a person's life would, as Thomas Hobbes suggested, be "nasty, brutish, and short."[2] Once those needs are fulfilled, we hunger for the approval of others. We come to understand that *no man is an island.* John Donne in his famous poem told this. Similarly, Aristotle proposed that man is a social animal when he wrote in his *Politics*[3]

> Man is by nature a social animal; an individual who is unsocial naturally and not accidentally is either beneath our notice or more than human. Society is something that precedes the individual. Anyone who either cannot lead the common life or is so self-sufficient as not to need to, and therefore does not partake of society, is ...a beast.

As we approach Maslow's higher levels of need motivation becomes increasingly focused on our particular idiosyncratic individuality. We yearn for the approval of ourselves, we yearn to satisfy the desire for self esteem. The particular nature of self esteem varies from one individual to the next. No man may be an island, yet every person is immersed in a sea that defines the boundaries of his or her own distinctiveness. Sonny Steele's self esteem depended on his decision to reject corporate control of the horse Rising Star. David's self esteem depended on his decision to go to New York, accept corporate control, and work on the Ford account.

Rousseau[4] as well as Freud[5] told us that civilized, i.e social, existence where man cannot freely fulfill his natural impulse to indeed live as a particular unique *island* in one way or another, is an obstacle to happiness. According to Maslow, the need for admiration of self eclipses the need for the admiration of others once the approval of others has been achieved. When others respect you your motivational drive focuses increasingly on the need to respect yourself. Sonny Steele decides that he does not need the admiration of people who see his picture on a box of breakfast cereal. David decides that he does not need the admiration of his friends who looked up to him when he decided to leave Los Angeles to "touch an Indian" …to live the life of a *free spirit.*

What made David, in *Lost in America*, feel comfortable in his own skin, his role as a corporate functionary, would never have done the same for Sonny Steele, in *Electric Horseman*. The authentic David characterizes the archetype of *organization man*. Sonny fits another variety of self, the rugged individual archetype of *cowboy.* The *ethic* of Davids corporate firm is the same as that of Sonney Steele's. It is the ethic of obedience to the boss. The *morality* of David, however is significantly different than that of Sonny.

The highest rung on Maslow's ladder of needs is the need for self-actualization. *Actualization* here can be taken as achievement, and *self* means just that. Self actualization accordingly means the achievement of self.

Clearly there is no difference at all between Maslow's psychologically derived notion of self-actualization and Aristotle's philosophically based proposal[6] that happiness results from:

> What is always chosen as an end in itself and never as a means to something else [but rather] is called final in an unqualified sense. This description seems to apply to happiness above all else: for we always choose happiness as an end in itself and never for the sake of something else.

Looking at what Aristotle says about happiness through the lens of Maslow's notions of motivation, we can take it that the *end* that is an *end it itself* is the goal of self-actualization.

If we need even more clarification on the meaning of the *achievement of self* we can turn to Robert Persig's proposal[7] concerning the very opposite of the happy state of self actualization: "...(T)hat strange separation of what man is from what man does (to find) some clues as to what the hell has gone wrong..." Self actualization is achieved when what we *do* is in harmony with what it is we *are*.

Maslow's hierarchy of needs starts off with identifying needs which drive motivation that is common to all and step by step climbs to the level where individual differences account for differences in motivation. The quest for happiness is driven by individual preference for (according to Aristotle) "what is chosen as an end in itself." Different people chose different ends. There are different *strokes* for different *folks*.

Given that the quest for individual happiness, i.e. self-actualization, is not the same for every self, then, it follows that morality which is determined by the inner voice which tells us what is virtuous and what is not is also determined by the unique nature of each individual's soul. Sonny Steele and David or for that matter Willy Keith's father in the *Caine Mutiny* story were members of the same society. A dominant norm of that society was that material welfare and financial status is an indicator of what is good, what is virtuous. Willy's father as well as David accepted this notion of virtue. Sonny did not.

The questions then become:

- How does each individual acquire his or her own sense of virtue?
- What *is virtue?*

These matters are investigated in Plato's description of a dialogue between Socrates and his friend Meno in his treatise *Meno.*[8]

The focus of Socrates' and Meno's discussion is Meno's desire to have Socrates tell him whether or not virtue can be taught. Meno's quest for the answer to this question is relevant to the discussion of the relationship between happiness and virtue so far. If virtue can be taught, then the difference between what is bad and what is good is determined by the learning we experience as a child, as a student, as a member of an organization, and as a member of society. If virtue cannot be taught, then the matter is more complicated than conceiving of virtue as conforming to those values which are *taught.*

As Plato describes the dialogue between Socrates and Meno it becomes apparent that Meno's question is of significant interest to Socrates. The question of the nature of virtue and whether or not it was a possible subject of instruction, arose from the teaching of the Sophists in ancient Greece, free-lance professors who traveled from city to city making a living out of a recent demand for education. Socrates believed that the Sophists were on the wrong track when it comes to teaching the difference between right and wrong and this is revealed by his conversation with Meno.

The dialogue starts with Meno's question to Socrates. "Is virtue something that can be taught?" Socrates speculates that there may be one single quality that explains all there is to know concerning what virtue is and Meno tries to sum this notion up by stating "It must be simply the capacity to govern men, if you are looking for one quality to cover all the instances." Meno speculates that the quality of justice, then, explains what virtue is. Socrates corrects him by pointing out that roundness is a shape and that "there are other shapes as well." He goes on to suggest that in his opinion "courage is a virtue and [so are] temperance and wisdom and dignity and many other things." It seems as though the concept of virtue cannot be captured by one singular phenomenon no more that the concept of shape can be captured by one singular contour. Socrates' teaching point here is that if virtue could be understood by understanding one singular phenomenon then it would be the same for everybody and Socrates refutes this notion.

Rather than continue on a track that seems to be going nowhere, Socrates leaves the question "What is virtue?" on the table and shifts the focus of the conversation back to Meno's original query concerning whether or not virtue can be taught.

Socrates gets to the crux of the matter when he tells Meno that "...the soul has learned everything.." and that seeking and learning are in fact nothing but recollection." He demonstrates the veracity of this by teasing out mathematical truth from a slave boy.

Socrates starts out by asking the boy if he knows that a square has four equal sides. The boy answers "Yes." With further questioning the boy correctly notes that if each side of the square is two feet long the area of the square will be four. As Socrates' questioning continues the boy comes to the correct conclusion that if the two foot long sides of the square are doubled to the length of four, the area of the square increases not to twice as much as the original square but to four times as much. The area of the new square the boy realizes is sixteen. So the mathematical knowledge of the boy is not determined by a teaching process, it is determined by questioning which demonstrates that the knowledge was there all along.

The idea that learning is a matter of recollection is also expressed by the plot of the *Groundhog Day* film. Phil learns about what it takes for him to be happy, what it takes for him to be virtuous, by recalling all the experience of the repeated days that he has been afforded by the fantasy of the story. Similarly, Scrooge, in Dickens' *Christmas Story* becomes a virtuous man as he is forced to recollect his past when he comes into contact with the *ghost of Christmas past.*

Socrates goes on to ask the slave boy increasingly complex questions that the boy has trouble dealing with. Socrates speculates that this creates discomfort and the discomfort will encourage the boy to continue to explore matters by questioning himself.

In the end of the dialogue Socrates comes to two conclusions. First of all, he points out that "...virtue will be acquired neither by nature or by teaching. Whoever has it gets it by divine dispensation..." Finally he tells Meno that "...we shall not understand the truth of the matter until, before asking how men get virtue, we try to discover what virtue is...."

How can all of this psychology proposed by Maslow and philosophy advocated by Socrates help us discover our distinctive authentic selves? How can we determine what that inner self is telling us about its unique sense of the difference between right and wrong?

The first step would be to listen to Maslow and understand that there are *different strokes for different folks.* The first step is to listen to yourself. The moral imperative that influenced me to cheat computer driven management control in the case of the shipyard overhaul would not be the same imperative for as everyone else.

The issue of whether or not there is a singular morality which should define a singular virtue is relevant to the distinction between differing doctrines of religious belief, as well as the vagaries of philosophy, political, and economic ideology. The morality of the Muslim is not the same as that of the Hindu. The moral philosophy of the Marxist is not the same as that of the Capitalist.

The virtue of particular set of values is a macro issue. The variability of coherent systems of values lies at the heart of the eternal conflict which characterizes the human condition, especially the condition of war. During the crusades the morality of Islam clashed with the morality of Christianity. During the *cold* war and its *hot* cousins in Vietnam and Korea the philosophy of communism quarreled with that of capitalism. More recently the extreme fundamentalist element of Muslim religion clashes with that of every other religion.

Religion notwithstanding, philosophers of all stripes have been searching for the *ultimate universal* truth that can capture *the ultimate universal* morality for thousands of years and have not found *it.*

As we seek to discover the morality and the virtue of our authentic selves we are dealing with the micro issue of *individual* happiness. If we focus exclusively on the eternal veil of tears that seems to characterize the eternal condition of humanity, if we accept the notion without any reservation that *no man is an island,* we construct a significant obstacle to the attainment of our own happiness. In this way we can risk sailing past the metaphorical tropical island, the paradise of our own bliss.

Whether knowledge, including knowledge of self, is given to us by "divine inspiration" as Socrates suggests, or from the formation of frames of reference and understanding which result from our own experience, as theories of *sensemaking* explained by Karl Weick tell us,[9] makes no difference to our discussion here. Either way, the point is that the practice of the art of living requires inspiration that comes from the teaching of *ourselves* rather than the instruction of others.

An important step on the road to self understanding is the conduct of a conversation with your inner self, the same sort of conversation that Socrates had with the slave boy. There is no doubt that we talk to ourselves in one way or another anyway. This conversation should start with relevant *Socratic,* i.e. leading and at times uncomfortable, questions. These questions can tease out answers which reveal the nature of our own morality. The answers that we come up with will change from time to time. Short of having achieved security needs we will have a tendency to go along with our organizational purposes unquestioningly. When we have climbed Maslow's ladder to the level of self-esteem we should be able to march to the beat of our own drum rather than that of our organization. This ladder is at times shaky and at times firm.

The path to happiness by way of self discovery not a straight line Gertrude Stein is reported to have said that "There is no answer, there never has been an answer, the never will be an answer — that's the answer." If we apply that conviction to the notion of the art of living as a *process* rather than a *product* we can accept Socrates' admonition to live an examined life and accept that this examination should be continuous—*approaching* a destination of self understanding and resultant happiness rather than arriving at a final journeys end.

Continuous self examination requires continuous questioning. The following chapter proposes various questions that may lead to answers that reveal self understanding.

Chapter Nineteen

The Conversation

Moral courage is courage in the presence of responsibility, whether before the judgment seat of an external authority or before that of the internal authority of conscience.

Karl Von Clausewitz

A good start at self examination would be to ask yourself the question *"Where am I on Maslow's hierarchy of needs?"*

For most people graduating from college and seeking employment, motivation is dominated by security needs: food, shelter, and safety. Of course, these are not our only needs. As we leave the womb of *alma mater* we do want to be admired by others and to feel a sense of self esteem. Nevertheless, the initial focus of our attention is economic self sufficiency. With our feet planted firmly on this level of Maslow's hierarchy of needs it is logical and rational to lean toward cooperation and away from defection when organizational purpose conflicts with that of ourselves.

In the *Lost in America* story David and Linda in a misguided attempt to find themselves find that they are on the lowest rung on Maslow's hierarchy of needs. With David earning a pittance as a crossing guard and Linda helping Skippy to manage a fast food restaurant (in their own words) they decide to "...go to New York and eat shit." They decide that their morality at this point should be driven by the spare state of their earning capacity.

As security needs become increasingly satisfied and as we learn more and more from experience about the nature of our individual *strokes* we can start to listen more intently to the beat of the *drum* that beats out the rhythm of those strokes.

Lieutenant Colonel Ben Gaitley in the *Twelve O'clock High* film starts out by exhibiting what General Savage calls "A yellow streak a mile wide." Gaitley is the bomber group's most experienced pilot, yet he has avoided flying assignments probably because, as Savage believes, he fears exposing himself to danger. Savage relieves Gaitley from his ground duties as second in command and assigns him to the job of pilot in command of a group of misfit crewmen. Savage names Gaitley's plane the "Leper Colony" and has this painted on the nose of his bombers.

When Gaitley's plane is severely damaged by enemy fire he is forced to ditch in the English Channel. He suffers a broken back and is hospitalized in severe pain. Savage, now much more respectful of Gaitley, visits him in the hospital. Savage asks Gaitley if he needs anything. Gaitley squinting with pain and tearing up replies, "No thank you General. I have everything I need." Gaitely has progressed from the (survival) need to stay alive to the need for the esteem of his fellow officer. He is one step higher on Maslow's ladder of motivation and one step closer to understand the his authentic self.

Jonathan E. in the *Rollerball* story is as close to achieving a state of self actualization as we can imagine. He has every physical and economic comfort one might desire, including the company of a series of beautiful women. He has the esteem of thousands of fans as well as his team mates. He is more than satisfied by his skill and achievement as an heroic athlete. When the corporation demands his retirement he refuses to do so. His defection is motivated by the fact that what he *is,* a Rollerball athlete, is the same as what he does.

Another question to ask yourself is *Where am I with respect to the extent of organizational socialization?*

As we become a member of an organization we are encouraged to take on the values of that system, i.e. to accept the process of socialization. This is a process that is necessary if the organization is to function smoothly and effectively. The attempt to socialize employees is a primary leadership function of those at the top of the organization's hierarchy.

It is evident that a process of organizational socialization starts during education. My education at the Naval Academy was more than just a learning experience. It was an experience designed to encourage me to accept the values of the Naval service, i.e. organization. In my first week as a student I was expected to answer the question "How long have you been in the Navy" with

All me bloomin' life, sir
Me mother was a mermaid, me father was King Neptune
I was born on the crest of a wave and rocked in the
cradle of the deep
Seaweed and barnacles are me clothes.
Every tooth in me head is a marlinspike
The hair on me head is hemp
Every bone in me body is a spar and when I spits,
I spits tar
I'se hard I am I are

The message is obvious. You may be new to us, nevertheless, we expect you to behave as though you have been here all your *bloomin' life*. We expect you to already be an *old salt*. We expect you immediately to take on all the values that we have acquired over many years.

Those values were expressed in the poem I was required to read and to memorize, a poem which specified *The Laws of the Navy*. Of the many stanzas, this one captures the essence of the process of socialization, a process that was a central theme of my four years at Annapolis on the banks of the Severn River.

On the strength of one link in the cable
Dependeth the might of the chain
Who knows when thou may'st be tested
So live that thou bearest the the strain

I was not only expected to already have achieved the status of old salt. I was moreover to consider my self to be one link in a *cable* that was the *chain* of human endeavor designed to fulfill the purposes of the organization. It does not take much in the way of imagination or analytical skill to understand that the link is me and the chain is the organization. If the chain breaks because I cannot bear the strain between my own purposes and those of the organization then the whole system will fail and it will be *my* fault.

The process of socialization that I experienced at the Naval Academy was not at all unique. The same sort of socialization process infuses a quite different set of values in students at the Harvard School of Business. Philip Delves Broughton wrote about his experience there in his *Ahead of the Curve: Two Years at Harvard Business School* [1]. Broughton tells us that "...in the first few weeks we struggled to learn the functional areas of business....the struggle to find the 'right' jobs became a separate education in itself...." He goes on to describe his "..experience in this cauldron of capitalism." The values of capitalism preached at the Harvard Business School are quite different from the values of devotion to service advocated at the Naval Academy.

Notwithstanding the stark difference between the role of Naval Officer and that of Business Executive, or my own continuing attachment to the former and irrational disdain for the latter, students at both places are socialized to enter life after graduation primed to join organizations where the values they took on in school will be useful to their organization. If there were an equivalent of the *Laws of the Navy* poem at Harvard Business School it might read

The strength of your learning to know
Will keep you from falling below

So work on the cases
Win all power races
Then go out and earn lots of dough

Closely related to the concept of socialization is the notion that all of us have a *zone of indifference*. This idea was the proposed by Chester I. Barnard in his *The Function of the Executive*[2]. Barnard was an American business executive and author of pioneering work in organization theory. His book is widely assigned in university courses in management and organization theory.

Barnard suggested that executives should issue orders to subordinates that were in their *zone of indifference*, orders that would be accepted unquestioningly and without resistance. In this way commands from above would be accepted without the questioning of authority and without the need to provide costly incentives to motivate employees to conform to organizational norms of obedience. When the mandate, either explicit or implicit, of higher authority is outside of a subordinate's zone of indifference, when subordinates are not at all indifferent to orders from above, it becomes increasingly likely that they will act in a rebellious manner or at least resist compliance.

Orders that are issued inside of a subordinate's zone of indifference do not require material incentives like overtime pay or increased salary. In this way managers, according to Barnard, should confine their control of subordinates to demands that are inside of their *zone of indifference*. In this way organizational efficiency would be maintained at a high level. More to the point, the manager gets more *production* at less *cost*.

The questioning of our own extent of socialization can be further explored as we ask ourselves, *How wide is my zone of indifference?*

A wide zone means that you will readily and unquestioningly accept the values and the mandates of the organization, that you are socialized to a great extent. A narrow zone means that you will question organizational values and resist compliance to managerial control efforts to which you are not at all indifferent. In this case your socialization is far from complete.

In the *Network* story the person at the top of the hierarchy, Mr. Jensen, wants to keep Howard Beale on the air to preach the ideology of capitalism and globalism. He wants Howard to act as a tool of his mega organization rather than as a professional member of the journalism community and an employee of the TV station news department. He wants to use Howard as a *human resource.* Howard accepts this role just as he previously accepted the role of a showman who chases ratings rather than a journalist who informs the public. When Howard's News Division colleagues child him with his compliance to the will of his seniors, he replies with "That's my job you are messing with." Howard sees himself as a resource to be used by Mr. Jensen and the organization. He is socialized to accept the values of the World Wide Corporation. His zone of indifference is very wide. His motivation is quite low on Maslow's hierarchy...at the level of survival.

Max Schumaker, in the same film story, on the other hand, is socialized as a professional journalist. When his boss, Frank Hackett wants to run the network news program as a profit center which chases ratings, rather than an organization that provides a service to viewers, Max refuses to accept orders from the top. Max has not been well socialized into the network as a ratings maximizing profit making organization. His zone of indifference is quite narrow.

As we pay attention to our own behavior relative to the extent of our socialization and the width of our *zone of indifference* we start to make more sense of what it is we do and come one step closer to understanding what it is we are.

Another question to ask yourself is *Do I see the situation at hand as one which calls for me to act in a way that is useful to the organization or does the situation demand that I act in accordance with an absolute sense of what is acceptable to me and what is not?*

Here our self understanding is informed by two philosophers with two opposing points of view. Jeremy Bentham, a philosopher of the school of utilitarianism, proposed that behavior is justified when it results in the accomplishment of *useful* desired objectives[3]. For Bentham the answer to the the question, "Is it right or wrong?" is "It depends."

To the contrary, Emanuel Kant tells us that morality should not be based on a situational contingency. Kant came up with the idea of a categorical imperative. He perceived *the good* in terms of absolute rather than relative criteria.[4]

As we make decisions in response to our day-to-day working experiences and scrutinize our own reaction to various situations, we might discern whether or not we are leaning toward the utilitarian philosophy of Bentham or acting from a sense of categorical imperative as proposed by Kant. Are we going along to get along to get along? Do we satisfy the needs of the boss or are we marching to the well defined, i.e. categorical, beat of our own drum when that beat is not in step with that of the organization?

Such philosophical based self examination brings closer to recognizing the state of our socialization, the width of our zone of indifference, and our position on Maslow's hierarchy of needs. All that helps us to understand the nature of our authentic self and the extent to which the work we do is our natural work.

If Sonny Steele would have ridden Rising Star in the Las Vegas trade show as directed, his behavior would have been useful to the corporation and in one sense useful to himself. His employment and high salary would have continued. On the other hand his behavior, the rescue of the horse from his status as a tool of the corporation was categorically unacceptable to Steele. Emanuel Kant would have approved.

As a junior officer serving on the accident board in the case of Spangle Twelve, cooperating with the officer in charge would have been useful to the squadron leadership and useful to myself. The squadron commanding officer would have been saved from the possibility of being charged with poor leadership and management that contributed to the tragedy. I would have avoided being perceived as a disloyal subordinate. On the other hand, the trauma of the death of my mates and my desire to help prevent such disaster in the future convinced me categorically to defect.

The wake up call for Sonny informed him about his own soul. He became aware of his authentic self when when push came to shove in Las Vegas as he met Rising Star and identified with the plight of the horse. As he Sonny walks off into an uncertain future he does so as a man where there is little if any conflict between what it is he does and what it is he is.

Similarly, as I defected from cooperating with the desires of my senior, I decided that purposeless loss of life was a category of event that was under no circumstances acceptable to me. I walked away from the Spangle Twelve experience with a good deal of self understanding. I was encouraged for the rest of the many years of my naval career to lean toward resisting orders from higher ups when those orders conflicted senselessly with the norm of the value of human life[5].

In the *Twelve O'clock High* story General Savage certainly did not relish the death of his subordinates. Nevertheless, he accepted the fact that, as he told his men, "Some of us are going to have to die." In peacetime circumstances Savage might have felt otherwise. In the wartime situation, however, the loss of life was a necessary, even a *useful*, cost of doing business. General Pritchard's desire to accept that the men should fly until they died resulted from his perception that the strategy of daylight precision bombing was useful to the continued existence of the Army Air Force as an organization and that the Army Air Force was useful to American society. In this case, the ethics of the organization specified the acceptability of the loss of life and the morality of Savage and Pritchard followed the mandate of that ethic. Jeremy Bentham would have approved.

The point here is not that Sonny Steele was right and the Generals were wrong or even the other way around. It is that making sense of ourselves, understanding ourselves, involves observing our own behavior when we confront a complex situation at hand. Do we desire absolute adherence to a hard and fast, i.e. categorical, imperative or do we prefer to take action that is practical and expedient to ourselves and to our organization? And if indeed we desire to succumb to a categorical imperative, what exactly *is* that absolute line that will will not cross.

Chapter Twenty

After All Is Said

*"I would urge each individual to avoid total involvement in
any organization."*

*Clark Kerr, as Chancellor of
the University of California, Berkeley*

What has been said in these pages is that working life should be a journey
of self discovery, that this discovery is the essential factor that determines
the capacity to happily integrate the mandates of organizational purpose
and the calling of one's authentic self.

Self understanding empowers us to practice the art of living. Various
suggestions have been made with respect to strategies and tactics that
can aid in the discovery of self. Paying very close attention to what it
is we say and what it is we do, for example, can help us to make sense
of our self. This tactic relies on ideas as disparate in time and method
as the recently developed social science principles of *sensemaking* (see
chapter eight) and the ancient philosophical proposition of Socrates that
the unexamined life is not worth living. Self examination leads to self
understanding.

The discovery of ones' authentic self, moreover, is important because
of the dual nature of what it means to be a human being, our outer apparent persona, the face we show to the world and to ourselves, and
the inner not so apparent spirit that forms the structure of our unique

individuality. Here again, a concept that is relevant to the theme of this book is revealed by templates of truth that are stamped by very different ways of knowing: ancient religions that specify the human soul as a critical component of human nature and the modern science of psychology which tells us that it is the dual structures of the conscious and the subconscious that determines our behavior. Both ancient theology and modern science help us to understand what it means to *be* a human being.

None of this would be relevant to our quest for happiness if it were not for the fact of life that the human condition, it seems, can put us in a position where our outer recognizable self comes into conflict with our inner authentic self, where our soul bumps us against our personality. This problem can surface in many ways because of the complexity of our human experience. The aspect of human experience that I have focused on here is life at work.

Of course, we experience more aspects of life than our work. The focus on the relationship between work and happiness in these pages emphasizes our involvement in the workplace because it is this role that is crucial to the development of the way we perceive our identity, the way we come to understand our authentic self.

The gentleman who cares for the health of my horses, dog, and cats is a son, a father, and a husband. When asked the question, however, "What are you?" his answer is invariably "a veterinarian." My partner in life, Kit, is a mother, a wife, a sister, a daughter, and a grandmother. When asked the question, however, "What are you?" her answer is "a published writer of mystery novels." There was a time in my own life that I went out of my way to tell people that I was a "pilot" and now I often introduce myself in one way or another as a "teacher." Our role as a worker is a dominant factor in the way we conceive of the purpose of our lives and the way we perceive our identity.

In the workplace, obstacles to the integration of the dual elements of what it means to be a human being, our hidden from sight inner soul and our discernible personality, can become problematical. This is because the purposes of our organization include goals other than the satisfaction of our own purpose, our own needs. (see chapter two). The cause of Sonny Steele's unhappiness as described in chapter eleven is that the corporation *uncowboyed* him. The cause of Jonathan E's happiness as described in chapter six is that he was able to overcome the corporation's attempt to steal his identity as a Rollerball champion. We tend to think of identify theft resulting from thieves becoming aware of our social security number, our credit card information, our bank account data, and our on-line computer passwords. It is, however, our organization which can be an even more invidious scoundrel who purloins our identity.

Central to what has been said in these pages is the relationship between purpose and happiness. Purpose is conceived of as the end objective in a chain of means and ends. We attend college to get an education. That education makes it possible to gain employment. Employment results in the economic capability to support a desired life style, and that life style in the best of circumstances accomplishes what we perceive is the purpose of all the means that we have employed in a chain of means and ends. It is Aristotle who relates this chain of means and ends conception to a useful definition of happiness. He tells us that happiness is the result of goals that are pursued as ends in and of themselves rather than means to an end.

Willie Keith's father in Wouk's *The Caine Mutiny* explains to his son that his unhappiness is the result of the pursuit of the objective of lofty socioeconomic status as a physician to the rich rather than assuming the role of a scientist who seeks to accomplish the goal of finding a cure for cancer. This work would have been a satisfying end in and of itself. His desire to satisfy the life style required by his wife was not a soul satisfying natural end in and of itself but a means to the spurious end of a tranquil married relationship. Doctor Keith has achieved tranquilly, but not happiness. The strategy that Doctor Keith on his deathbed recommends to his son is to find his natural work, work that would be an end in and of itself, an end that would be in harmony with Willie's authentic individuality, his own particular humanity. (see chapter three).

Finally, all that has been said is captured by William Whyte's admonition in his *The Organization Man* [1]. He tells us that we have to face the fact that in seeking to attain a *sham* peace of mind by unquestioningly *worshiping* our organization we fail to stay on a path that leads to happiness.

> The fault is not in organization, in short; it is in our worship of it. It is in our vain quest for a Utopian equilibrium, which would be horrible if it ever did come to pass.....There must always be, and it is the price of being an individual that we must face these conflicts....in seeking an ethic that offers a spurious peace of mind, thus do we tyrannize ourselves.

Notes

CHAPTER ONE

1. Aristotle. *Nichomachean Ethics.* New York: Macmillian, 1962.
2. Wouk, H. *The Caine Mutiny.* Boston: Little Brown, 1951, pp.63-66.
3. Tolstoy, L. *The Death Of Ivan Ilych.* New York: Penguin, 1960.
4. Taylor, F. *The Principles of Scientific Management.* New York: ReadaClassic, 1911
5. Chaplain (1936).
6. Mayo, E. *The Social Problems of an Industrial Civilization.* Boston: Harvard Business School Press, 1945.
7. Whyte, W. *The Organization Man.* Philadelphia: University of Pennsylvania Press, 2002.
8. Plato. *Five Dialogues.*Indianapolis: Hackett, 2002.
9. Plato, 2002.
10. Plato, *Republic.* Indianapolis: Hackett, 1992.
11. Aristotle, 1962
12. Rousseau, *A Discourse on Inequality.* London: Penguin, 1984.
13. Nietzsche, F. *Beyond Good and Evil.* London: Dover, 1997.
14. Freud, S. *Civilization and Its Discontents.* Mansfield, CT: Martino, 2010
15. Rousseau, 1984
16. Persig, R. *Zen And The Art of Motorcycle Maintenance.* New York:Bantam, 1975

CHAPTER TWO

1. Hobbes, T. *Leviathan.* Hertfordshire: Wordsworth, 1987
2. Gerth, H. *From Max Weber: Essays In Sociology.* Oxford: Oxford University Press, 1946

3. King (1949)
4. Stone (1987)
5. Hackford (1997)

CHAPTER THREE

1. McCarthy, C. *All The Pretty Horses.* NewYork: Knopf, 1992.
2. Plato. *Protagoras And Meno.* London: Penguin, 1956.
3. Freud, S. *The Basic Writings of Sigmund Freud,* New York: Random House, 1965.
4. Jung, C. *The Portable Jung,* New York:Penguin, 1971.
5. Herbert, G. *The Complete English Poems,* New York, Penguin, 1991.
6. Wouk, H. *The Caine Mutiny.* Boston: Little Brown, 1951.
7. Tolstoy, L. *The Death Of Ivan Ilych.* New York: Penguin, 1960.

CHAPTER FOUR

1. Wouk, H. *The Caine Mutiny.* Boston: Little Brown, 1951
2. Tolstoy, L. *The Death Of Ivan Ilych.* New York: Penguin, 1960.
3. King (1949).
4. Orwell, G. *1984.* New York: Penguin, 1949.
5. Chaplain (1936).

CHAPTER FIVE

1. Lumet (1976).
2. Jewison (1975.
3. Easton, David. *A Framework for Political Analysis.* New York: Prentice Hall,1965.
4. Philip Kaufman (1983)
5. Easterly, W. *The Tyranny of Experts.* New York: Basic Books, 2014.
6. Siegel (1971)
7. Zinneman (1952)
8. Vidor (1949)

CHAPTER SIX

1. Jewison 1975)

CHAPTER SEVEN

1. Google, Inc. Human Resource Literature.
2. Levine, D. *Reuters News,* 2014.
3. Shah, A. *IDG News Service,* September 2, 2014.
4. R. Rashke. *The Killing of Karen Silkwood.* Ithaca: Cornell Paperbacks, 2000.
5. R. Rashke. *The Killing of Karen Silkwood: The Story Behind The Kerr-Mcgee Plutonium Case.* New York:Sphere Books, 1983.
6. Taylor, F. *The Principles of Scientific Management.* Eastford, CT:Marino Fine Books, 2014.
7. McGregor, D. *The Human Side of Enterprise* in Ott, J. (ed) *Classic Readings in Organizational Behavior.* Belmont: Wadsworth, 1996, pp. 57-62.
8. Chaplain (1936).
9. Mayo, E. *The Social Problems of an Industrial Civilization.* Boston: Harvard Business School Press, 1945.
10. —McGregor, 1996.
11. Ouchi.W. *Theory Z: How American Business Can Meet the Japanese Challenge.* Essex:Addison-Wesley,1981.
12. "The Rise of Workplace Spying", *The Week; The Best of the U.S. and International Media,* July 10, 2015, p. 11.
13. —"The Rise of Workplace Spying."

CHAPTER EIGHT

1. Kuhn, Thomas. *The Structure of Scientific Revolutions.* Chicago: The University of Chicago Press, 1962.
2. Weick, K. *Sensemaking in Organizations.* Thousand Oaks: Sage, 1995.
3. —Weick, 1995

CHAPTER NINE

1. Czarniawska-Joerges, B. *A Narrative Approach to Organization Studies*. Thousand Oaks: Sage, 1998.
2. Waldo, D. *The Novelist on Organization and Administration: An Inquiry Into the Relationship Between Two Worlds*. Berkeley: Institute of Governmental Studies, 1968
3. —Waldo 1968, pp.25.
4. —Waldo 1968, pp. 25.
5. Goodsell, C.N. and Murray, (eds) *Public Administration Illuminated and Inspired by the Arts*. New York: Praeger, 1995
6. —Goodsell and Murray.

CHAPTER TEN

1. Brooks (1985)

CHAPTER ELEVEN

1. Pollack (1979)
2. Olin (2001)

CHAPTER TWELVE

1. Dickens, C. *A Christmas Carol.* London: Chapman & Hall, 1843.
2. Ramis (1993)

CHAPTER THIRTEEN

1. Reiner (1992)
2. Festinger, L. *A Theory of Cognitive Dissonance.* Stanford CA:Stanford University Press, 1957.

3. Weick, K. *Sensemaking in Organizations*. Thousand Oaks: Sage, 1995.p.12

CHAPTER FOURTEEN

1. Landau, M. and Stout, R. Jr. *To Manage Is Not to Control: Or the Folly of Type II Errors* in Public Administration Review, March/April, 1979

CHAPTER FIFTEEN

1. Sloane, S. *Gold Stripe on a Jackass; The Quest for Moral Efficiency*. New York:Rowman and Littlefield, 2008.

CHAPTER SIXTEEN

1. Sloane, S. *Gold Stripe on a Jackass; The Quest for Moral Efficiency*. New York:Rowman and Littlefield, 2008.

CHAPTER SEVENTEEN

1. Kubrick (1968)

CHAPTER EIGHTEEN

1. Maslow A. *Motivation and Personality.* New York: Harper, 1954.
2. Hobbes, T. *Leviathan.* Indianapolis: Hackett Publishing, 1994.
3. Aristotle. *Politics. Chicago: University of Chicago Press, 2013.*
4. Rousseau, J. J. *A Discourse on Inequality.* London: Penguin Books, 1984.
5. Freud, S. *Civilization and Its Discontents.* New York:Norton, 1961.
6. Aristotle. *Nichomachean Ethics.* New York: Macmillian, 1962.

7. Pirsig, R. *Zen and the Art of Motorcycle Maintenance.* New York :William Morrow, 1974.
8. Plato, *Protagoras and Meno.* London: Penguin, 1956.
9. Weick, K. *Sensemaking in Organizations.* Thousand Oaks: Sage, 1995.

CHAPTER NINETEEN

1. Broughton, P.D. *Ahead of the Curve: Two Years at Harvard Business School.* New York: Penguin Books, 2008.
2. Barnard, C.I. *The Function of the Executive.* Cambridge: Harvard University Press, 1938.
3. Everett, C. W. *Jeremy Bentham*, London: Weidenfeld and Nicholson, 1966.
4. Aune, B. *Kant's Theory of Morals*, Princeton, NJ: Princeton University Press,1979.
5. Sloane, S. *Gold Stripe on a Jackass; The Quest for Moral Efficiency.* New York:Rowman and Littlefield, 2008.

CHAPTER TWENTY

1. Whyte, W. *The Organization Man.* Philadelphia: Simon and Schuster, 2002.

About the Author

Stephen Sloane, Ph.D., is a Professor Emeritus of Political Science and Public Administration at Saint Mary's College of California.

He is a graduate of:

- The U.S. Naval Academy (BS), where he has served as a member of the faculty.
- Harvard University (MPA), where he conducted a study of military professionalism as a John F. Kennedy Graduate School of Public Administration Research Fellow.
- The University of California, Berkeley (MA, Ph.D.), where as Research Fellow at the Institute for Governmental Studies he did ethnographic research while embedded with the San Francisco Police Department. He has also lectured at the University of California Haas School of Business.

His current research interests deal with the role of professionals in modern organizations, novels and film as sources of ideas that contribute to the understanding of organizational systems, critical management studies, and ethics.

As a career naval officer he attained the rank of Captain, having been assigned to various duties in aviation squadrons, aboard ship, and at shore stations.

In addition to his teaching and scholarship activity, he is an equestrian, has published widely on the subject of the horse-human connection, and has provided therapeutic riding experiences for people with disabilities.

He lives in California with his wife, Kit Sloane, the author of a popular mystery novel series.